Contents

Introduction

All eyes turned to the trees. A horseman rode out, toward the Roman army. There was something strange about the way he was riding. Maximus was the first to understand . . .

As the horse came closer, the other men could see what had happened. The Roman messenger was tied to his horse. His head had been cut off. Maximus knew now what he had to do. Life was suddenly simple.

General Maximus, Commander of the Roman Army of the North, fights his last battle in the war against Germania. Then, he hopes to return to his farm and his family in Spain.

But there are many serious problems in Rome and Emperor Marcus Aurelius knows he will soon die. Maximus realizes that he must perform another duty for the Emperor before he can go home. He knows it will not be easy, and he is right. Soon he is fighting for his life again, first as a prisoner, then a slave, and finally as a gladiator.

One thought keeps Maximus alive: that he will finally meet and kill the man he hates most—the new Emperor, Commodus.

The book, *Gladiator*, was written by Dewey Gram. The screenplay by David Franzoni, John Logan, and William Nicholson was made into a very successful movie. The movie stars Russell Crowe as Maximus and Joaquin Phoenix as Commodus. British actor Oliver Reed (Proximo) died before the movie was finished, although almost all his scenes had been completed.

On film and on paper, *Gladiator* is a very exciting story.

Chapter 1 Farmer and Soldier

At the height of its power, the great Roman Empire stretched from the deserts of Africa to the borders of northern England. Over one quarter of the world's population lived and died under the rule of the Caesars.★

In the winter of A.D.† 180, Emperor Marcus Aurelius's twelve-year war against the people of Germania was coming to an end. There was one last battle to win. Then there would be peace across the Roman Empire.

◆

The man walked through the sun-warmed Spanish field, his hand touching the wheat. He looked past apple trees to a farmhouse. He heard a child laughing somewhere near. A bird flew onto the branch of a tree close to him and they looked at each other. The man smiled.

Suddenly, the sound of shouts and horses frightened the bird and it flew up into the air. The noise broke through the man's daydream and he came back to the real world with a crash. He was not dressed in farmer's clothes, as he had imagined, but in the proud armor of the Roman army. The field was burnt and muddy from battle, without a green leaf on it.

Beyond the tree line ahead, somewhere in the forest, the German armies were preparing to attack again. The man knew that behind him an enormous army waited. The Roman army, 40,000 men, his army. Maximus the farmer was Maximus the Commanding General of the Army of the North for one more

★ Caesar: the title given to the Roman Emperor.
† A.D.: after the birth of Christ.

battle. One last battle, and then he could go home to Spain.

He turned his horse and rode back to his men. Thirty-year-old Maximus was a great general—a man they could trust. He moved among them, checking that they were ready for battle. He looked back frequently to the line of trees.

Some of his officers were warming themselves around a fire, and Maximus joined them.

"Still nothing?" he asked Quintus, his second-in-command.

Quintus shook his head. "He's been gone for almost two hours," he said. "Why are they taking so long? They only have to say yes or no."

A young officer gave Maximus a bowl of hot soup. He drank it slowly as they talked, always keeping one eye on the line of trees.

"Snow in the air," said Maximus. "I can smell it."

"Anything's better than this German rain," Quintus said, looking out at the mud in front of his men.

Suddenly, there was a shout. "He's coming!"

All eyes turned to the trees. A horseman rode out, toward the Roman army. There was something strange about the way he was riding. Maximus was the first to understand.

"They say no," he said.

As the horse came closer, the other men could see what had happened. The Roman messenger was tied to his horse. His head had been cut off. Maximus knew now what he had to do. Life was suddenly simple.

Far away, at the edge of the trees, a German chief appeared. In one hand he was holding the head of the messenger. He screamed his anger at the Roman army, then threw the head toward them.

Maximus's men stared back and waited for their general's order to attack.

◆

Several carriages traveled along the road toward the battle area, protected by Roman soldiers. Inside the first carriage were the royal family—the Emperor's son and daughter. Twenty-eight-year-old Commodus and his beautiful older sister Lucilla were dressed in rich, warm clothes. They had left Rome two weeks before.

"Do you think he's really dying?" Commodus asked Lucilla.

"He's been dying for ten years," she replied.

"I think he's really sick this time. And he's sent for us." He pointed to the following carriages. "He sent for the senators, too. If he isn't dying, why does he want to see them?"

"Commodus, you're giving me a headache. Two weeks on the road with you is more than enough," said Lucilla, impatiently.

Commodus moved closer to her. "No, he's made his decision," he said. "He will name me as Emperor. And I know what I shall do first. I shall organize some games . . ."

"I shall have a hot bath," said Lucilla.

The carriage stopped. Commodus stepped down and spoke to one of the guards.

"We are almost there, sir."

"Good," said Commodus. "Bring me my horse."

Under his warm traveling coat Commodus was wearing Roman armor. He looked handsome and brave, the perfect picture of a new, young emperor. The guard brought Commodus his horse.

"Take me to my father. And take my sister to the camp." Commodus reached out a hand to Lucilla. "Kiss," he said, smiling like a little boy.

Lucilla brushed his fingers with her lips, then watched him ride away.

◆

Marcus Aurelius, Emperor of Rome, sat on his horse and stared at the army below. His hair and beard were white, but only his eyes really showed his age and state of health. Marcus knew he was dying and soon he must name the next emperor. But first, this battle must be won.

From another hill, Maximus also looked down onto the Roman army. His men were ready to fight.

The German soldiers started to move out from the trees. There were thousands of them, dressed in animal skins, shouting at their Roman enemies.

Maximus bent down from his horse and took some earth in his hands, as he did before every battle. Then he let it fall through his fingers. It was a sign his men had seen many times before and they knew what it meant. Maximus gave the command and a flaming arrow shot into the sky. Hundreds more followed.

Thousands of German soldiers rushed forward and met the first line of Romans. The air was filled with the sound of screaming as more arrows landed and men from both armies died terrible deaths.

Maximus led soldiers on horseback into the battle at the same time as 5,000 Roman foot soldiers moved forward from another side. Each man marched behind a large shield, each carried a sword. The Germans were caught between two walls of death. Above them the sky was full of flaming arrows. They were fighting for their lives.

Suddenly, Maximus was trapped between two Germans. He swung his sword around in a circle, striking both men dead. Then he rode forward again, and his sword cut through the enemy soldiers in his path.

Maximus's horse suddenly fell forward, a German sword in its neck. The General flew over his horse's head and crashed to the ground. There was danger all around him, but he continued fighting. He found the Roman flag, still in the hand of a dead soldier, and held it high. His men fought their way toward it and defended their position bravely.

More and more Roman soldiers moved forward onto the battleground. They were well-trained and had the best equipment and armor. The Germans were not as good as the confident Roman army and finally they began to tire. Maximus saw that he was winning and moved up a little higher on the hill. From there he could see and command his men better. The enemy began to lose confidence and some turned and ran. More joined them and soon the only Germans on the battlefield were dead or dying.

Maximus went back down and walked among them. As he stepped over bodies, he began to relax and let his sword arm fall to his side. Behind him, a dying German suddenly lifted himself from the ground and rushed forward with his sword. Maximus was calling an order to one of his officers when he saw the sudden look of terror on the officer's face and immediately swung his sword around, cutting off his attacker's head. There was so much power behind the sword that it flew from his hand and landed in a tree.

Maximus had no strength left to pull it out again. The battle had ended. As he looked at the dead around him, he could only think that his men had won, and he had lived.

Chapter 2   The Last Battle

Emperor Marcus Aurelius sat on his horse, on the top of the command hill, with guards on each side to protect him. He watched as the battle slowly progressed and it became clear that the Roman army had won. Marcus hoped it would be many years before they had to go to war again, certainly not before he died. He had no wish to see another battle. He turned to his guards. "I will leave now," he said. "I have seen enough."

Maximus looked at his sword in the tree. His face was covered with blood and mud. The beat of his heart was beginning to slow down as the noise of the battle became quieter. There were other sounds now—screams from the dying and cries for help.

A small bird flew down from the top of the tree and sat on Maximus's sword. Could it possibly be the same bird he had seen before the first explosion of battle? That seemed like a hundred years ago. He shook his head and reached for the sword. The frightened bird flew away as Maximus pulled his sword out of the tree.

Across the field, doctors were trying to help any Roman soldiers who were still alive. Other soldiers were walking slowly through the men on the ground, looking for Germans left alive and killing them quickly.

Maximus walked back toward the command point, sometimes stopping to speak to a dying soldier, sometimes calling for water or medical help. He came to a low hill where the bodies of Roman soldiers had been placed, side by side.

"Let the sun always be warm on your back," he said softly. "You've come home at last."

"You're a brave man, Maximus, and a good commander," said a voice behind him. "Let us hope it is for the last time."

Maximus turned and saw the Emperor. "There's no one left to fight, sir," he said.

"There are always people to fight. More glory."

"The glory is theirs, Caesar," said Maximus, looking at the lines of dead soldiers.

"Tell me," said Marcus. "How can I reward Rome's greatest general?"

"Let me go home," replied Maximus, quickly.

"Ah, home . . ." said Marcus. He gave his arm to Maximus, and they walked together back across the battlefield.

All eyes followed the long purple coat and white hair of their emperor. They could see that he moved slowly and with difficulty. He was clearly in pain. Most of the soldiers realized that they were probably seeing him for the last time. And they knew Rome was not likely to have such a good emperor again.

Marcus Aurelius and his general walked along the road, past lines of tired soldiers. Hundreds of men resting on a hill stood and raised their swords high in the air when they saw them pass.

"They honor you, Caesar," said Maximus.

"No, Maximus, I believe they honor *you*," replied the Emperor.

Maximus looked across at the crowd of brave men and raised his own sword. The men cheered him loudly.

Suddenly, Prince Commodus and his guards rode into view. When he heard the cheering and saw the reason for it, Commodus was filled with jealousy. Roman soldiers were honoring a Spaniard above the Emperor and his family—it was not right. But he tried to look pleased as he rode up to Marcus and Maximus.

"Have I missed the battle?" he said, jumping from his horse.

"You've missed the war," said Marcus. "We're finished here."

Commodus put his arms around his father. "Father, congratulations," he said. "I shall kill a hundred animals to honor your success."

"Let the animals live and honor Maximus," said Marcus. "He won the battle."

"General," Commodus said, turning to Maximus, "Rome salutes you, and I salute you as a brother." He opened his arms and put them around Maximus. "It has been too long since we last met. How long? Ten years, my old friend?" Commodus turned to Marcus. "Here, Father, take my arm."

Marcus let his hand rest on his son for a minute, then said, "I think maybe I should leave you now."

Commodus called for Marcus's horse and some of the guards ran forward to help him. The old man waved them away and looked at Maximus. Maximus came quickly to his side and helped him onto the horse. Without a word to his son he rode slowly away.

Commodus and Maximus stood together and watched the Emperor go, each thinking their own thoughts about him.

Marcus had won many battles for the glory of Rome, but Maximus would always remember him first as a good man.

Commodus's thoughts were very different. He was angry that his father had not put his arms around him. He was jealous because Maximus was asked to help Marcus onto the horse and the Emperor had spoken privately to him. He swung himself back onto his horse and rode away, followed by his guards.

◆

A city of hospital tents had been built. There were thousands of wounded Roman soldiers, and the doctors were busy all night. Maximus came out of one of the tents. He was sad that so many men were badly hurt, and he knew that many more would not live until morning.

He turned and walked back to the main camp. In the biggest tent many of the officers were celebrating. There was wine and food; they were laughing and shouting. These were the lucky men who had cheated death.

The Emperor sat in a chair in the center of the tent and received visitors. Two senators, Falco and Gaius, had just arrived.

"We greet you, Marcus Aurelius," Falco said. "And we bring greetings from Senator Gracchus. He waits to honor you when you return to Rome."

When Maximus entered the tent, officers came forward to meet him. Someone gave him wine, others held their hands out to him. Quintus stopped his conversation when he saw his friend.

"Still alive! The gods must love you!" they both said together, laughing. Maximus moved through the tent, with Quintus and some of his other officers following behind.

Through the forest of men Maximus could see Marcus Aurelius surrounded by a group of people. As he got nearer, he saw Commodus at the Emperor's side, with the two senators. Maximus paused to speak to another officer.

"Back to Rome now, General?" the man asked.

"I'm going home," Maximus said. "To my wife, my son, and my fields of wheat."

"Maximus the farmer!" Quintus said, laughing. "I still can't imagine that."

"Dirt washes off more easily than blood, Quintus," replied Maximus.

Commodus, Gaius, and Falco came toward Maximus.

"Here he is," said Commodus. "The hero of the war!"

Maximus was not happy that Commodus had said this in front of his brave officers. To him they were all heroes.

Commodus introduced the two senators. They were smart politicians and they saw that Maximus could have an interesting future in Rome. The real power was not with the Emperor. It was with whoever had control of the army.

Commodus led Maximus away to a quieter corner. He spoke softly. "Times are changing, General. I'm going to need good men like you."

"How can I help, sir?"

"You're a man who can command. You give orders, the men follow your orders, the battle is won." Commodus looked across at the senators. "We must save Rome from the politicians, my friend. Will you be with me when the time comes?"

"When your father allows me to go, I will return to Spain, sir," said Maximus.

"Home? Ah yes. But don't get too comfortable—I may call on you soon." Then, seeming suddenly to remember, Commodus said, "Lucilla is here. Did you know? She hasn't forgotten you—and now you are the great hero." He turned away to watch his father leaving the tent with his guards. "Caesar will sleep early tonight," he said.

9

When he turned back again, Maximus had gone. Commodus was anxious. Who did the great general really support? Could he be trusted? Commodus took some more wine and thought carefully about Maximus.

◆

Marcus's slaves helped him into the royal tent. Lucilla was already there.

"It's a pity I only have one son," Marcus said to her. "You would be a better Caesar than Commodus ... stronger. I wonder if you would also be fair?"

"I would be whatever you taught me to be," she replied, smiling. She came to his side and kissed him.

"How was the trip?" Marcus asked.

"Long. Boring. Why have I come?" asked Lucilla.

"I need your help," said her father. "With your brother. He loves you—he always has. Soon he is going to need you more than ever." Lucilla did not know what to say. "No more. It is not a night for politics," Marcus said. "It is a night for an old man and his daughter to look at the moon together. Let us pretend that you are a loving daughter and I am a good father."

Lucilla took his arm and they walked together into the cold night air. "This is a pleasant fiction," she said, smiling at him.

Lucilla understood him. She knew that her father would love to be just a simple old man sharing a little time with his daughter. But he was Emperor of Rome, and for him life was much more complicated.

◆

In the cold morning, at the edge of the forest, a group of men were training for battle. Commodus and his guards were practicing sword fighting, striking at small trees.

The young prince was proud of his body. He was strong and

healthy as a result of the strict training he did every morning. His training program was taken straight from the gladiator schools, where men learned to fight for their lives. His greatest wish was to fight against real gladiators, although he knew that his father would never allow it. Marcus had ended the tradition of gladiator fights in Rome.

Maximus passed by the small group of men in the early morning light and noticed that the Emperor's son was among them. He was not surprised. He had heard plenty of stories about Commodus, how strong and skilled he was. He had also heard that Commodus was a cruel man, but he tried not to believe that. There were always jealous people saying bad things about the royal family.

Maximus walked to Marcus's tent. The Emperor's guards let him through the entrance without any questions. They were expecting him.

Chapter 3 One More Duty

The only light in the Emperor's tent came from oil lamps. Marcus sat with his back to Maximus. He was writing his diary and at first he did not realize Maximus had arrived.

"Caesar. You sent for me," said Maximus. Marcus, lost in his thoughts, did not reply. "Caesar?" Maximus repeated.

"Tell me again, Maximus," Marcus said. "Why are we here?"

"For the glory of the Empire, sir."

At first he thought Marcus had not heard him. Then Marcus slowly got up from his desk and softly said, "Yes, I remember . . ."

He walked over to a large map of the Roman Empire and waved a hand across it. "Do you see it, Maximus? This is the world I have made. For twenty years I have tried to be a student of life and of men—but what have I really done?" He touched the map. "For twenty years I have fought and won battles. I have defended the Empire and increased it. Since I became Caesar I have only had four years of peace. And for what?"

"To make our borders safe," said Maximus. "To bring teaching and law."

"I brought the sword! Nothing more! And while I have fought, Rome has grown fat and diseased. I did this. And nothing can change the fact that Rome is far away and we shouldn't be here."

"But Caesar . . ." Maximus started, but Marcus interrupted him.

"Don't call me that," he said. "We have to talk together now. Very simply. Just as men. Can we do that?"

"Forty thousand of my men are out there now, freezing in the mud," said Maximus. "Eight thousand are wounded and two thousand will never leave this place. I won't believe they fought and died for nothing."

"What do you believe, Maximus?"

"That they fought for you—and for Rome," he replied.

"And what is Rome, Maximus? Tell me."

"I've seen too much of the rest of the world and I know it's cruel and dark. I have to believe that Rome is the light."

"But you have never been there," said Marcus. "You have not seen Rome as it is now."

Maximus had heard stories about Rome. People in the cities were hungry and food prices were much too high. Some Romans had become very rich, but most were poor. Bridges, roads, and ports all needed repairs, while tax money went into the pockets of the rich. There were many things wrong at the heart of the enormous empire.

"I am dying, Maximus. And I want to see that there has been some purpose to my life." Marcus sat down again. "It's strange. I think more about the future than the present. How will the world speak my name in future years?" He held out his hand to Maximus, who took it and came to sit next to Marcus.

"You have a son," said the Emperor. "You must love him very much. Tell me about your home."

"The house is in the hills above Trujillo," Maximus began. "It's a simple place, pink stones that warm in the sun. There's a wall, a gate, and a small field of vegetables." Maximus looked up and saw that the old man had closed his eyes as he listened. He was smiling. "Through the gate are apple trees. The earth is black, Marcus. As black as my wife's hair. And we grow fruit and vegetables. There are wild horses near the house—my son loves them."

"How long is it since you were last home?"

"Two years, two hundred sixty-four days—and one morning."

Marcus laughed. "I am jealous of you, Maximus. Your home is good—something to fight for. I have one more duty to ask of you before you go home."

"What would you like me to do, Caesar?"

"Before I die, I will give the people a final gift. An empire at peace should not be ruled by one man. I want to give power back to the Senate."

Maximus was shocked. "But sir, if no one man holds power, all men will reach for it."

"You're right. That is why I want you to become the Protector of Rome. Give power back to the people of Rome." Maximus said nothing. "You don't want this great honor?"

"With all my heart, no."

"That is why it must be you," Marcus replied.

"But what about Commodus?"

"Commodus is not a good man. I think you already know that. He must not rule. You are more of a son to me than he is." Marcus stood up. "Commodus will accept my decision—he knows the army is loyal to you."

13

A piece of ice struck Maximus's heart. "I need some time, sir," he said.

"Of course. By sunrise tomorrow I hope your answer will be yes. Now let me hold you as a son." Marcus put his arms around Maximus.

♦

Maximus left the Emperor's tent feeling anxious. One more duty, one he did not want—but could he refuse? He was a loyal soldier, loyal to Rome and to Caesar. He stood outside the tent trying to think clearly. Suddenly, there was a voice behind him.

"You are my father's favorite now."

Maximus turned and saw Lucilla. As their eyes met, a shock of emotion ran through them both.

"It was not always true," said Lucilla.

"Many things have changed since we last met," said Maximus, and he turned to walk away.

"What did my father want with you?"

"To wish me luck, before I leave for Spain," he replied.

"You're lying," said Lucilla. "I could always tell when you were lying. You're not very good at it."

"I was never as good as you, my lady."

Lucilla did not try to deny it. Again, Maximus tried to leave.

"Maximus, please . . . is it really so terrible to see me again?"

"No, I'm sorry. I'm tired from battle," he said.

"And you're upset to see my father so weak. Commodus expects our father to name him in a few days as the next Caesar. Will you be as loyal to him as you have been to Marcus?"

This was a difficult question, but Maximus never forgot that he was talking to one of the royal family.

"I will always be loyal to Rome," he said.

"Do you know I still remember you when I speak to the gods?" said Lucilla, smiling.

"I was sorry to hear of your husband's death. I understand you have a son."

"Yes," said Lucilla. "Lucius. He's almost eight years old."

"I, too, have a son who is eight years old."

They smiled at each other again.

"I thank you for your kind thoughts," said Maximus, and then he walked slowly back to his tent. Lucilla watched him go. Her thoughts were confused, and her emotions reminded her that she had once loved this man.

◆

Maximus sat in front of a low table in his tent. On the table were small wooden figures of his family—parents and grandparents. In the center, protected by the others, were the two smallest figures. These were his wife and child.

As he looked at his family, he tried to imagine what his father or grandfather would do in his situation. What would they decide? How would they advise him? He picked up the figure of his wife and kissed it.

"Cicero," he called out. Behind him, his servant Cicero appeared and gave him a drink. "Do you ever find it difficult to do your duty?" Maximus asked him.

Cicero, a tall, thin man with long hair, thought about the question for a few seconds. "Sometimes I do what I want to do, sir," he said. "The rest of the time I do what I have to do."

Maximus smiled. "We may not be able to go home," he said, sadly.

◆

Marcus Aurelius sat in his great tent, lit only by the light of a fire, and prepared himself to tell Commodus of his decision. Finally, he said, "You will do your duty for Rome."

Commodus stood in front of him, proud and tall, waiting to

15

hear his father name him as the next Caesar. "Yes, Father," he said.

"But you will not be Emperor," Marcus said.

Commodus froze as his future suddenly disappeared. "Who will take my place?" he asked.

"My power will pass to Maximus, to hold until the Senate is ready to rule. Rome will be a republic again. I can see that you are not happy, my son . . ."

"You break my heart," Commodus said. "I have tried to make you proud . . . but I could never do it. Why do you hate me so much? I only wanted to be your son, but I was never quite good enough." Marcus put his arms around his son, and Commodus cried. "Why does Maximus deserve this instead of me? Why do you love him more than me?"

His voice grew louder as he held his father's head tighter and tighter. Marcus could not breathe. He began to move, trying to get away, but Commodus held his father's face close against his chest. His strength was too great; Marcus could not escape. Commodus did not relax until he felt his father's body drop in his arms.

He placed him on the bed, dead. "You didn't love me enough," he said softly.

♦

Quintus woke Maximus in the middle of the night. Maximus realized immediately that there was trouble.

"The Emperor needs you," Quintus said. "It's urgent."

"What is it?" Maximus asked.

"They did not tell me," said Quintus.

They hurried to Marcus's tent together. At the entrance, the guards let them through without a word.

Inside, Maximus saw Commodus first. His face was white but showed no emotion. Lucilla stood in a corner of the tent, looking down at the floor. Then Maximus saw Marcus, lying on his bed. He knew immediately that he was dead.

16

"How did he die?" he asked.

"In his sleep," said Commodus. "The doctors say there was no pain."

Maximus looked at Lucilla, but she turned away. He walked to the bed, bent over Marcus, and kissed the top of his head. Then he stood and faced Commodus. Commodus looked back at him and held out his hand.

"Your Emperor asks for your loyalty," he said. "Take my hand, Maximus." Maximus understood the situation exactly. He knew, without a doubt, that Commodus had killed his father. "I shall only offer it once," said Commodus.

Maximus walked past him and out of the tent. Quintus already had his orders from the new Caesar. Commodus looked across at him and he followed his general out into the night.

Lucilla bent over her father and kissed him. Then she turned to her brother. Their eyes met. She hit his face twice, hard. He stepped back, shocked. Then she took his right hand, lifted it to her lips, and kissed it.

"I greet you, Caesar," Lucilla said without emotion.

◆

Back in his own tent, Maximus called to Cicero. "I must talk to the senators," he said. "Wake Gaius and Falco! I need their advice."

Quintus arrived just then, and caught the servant's arm to stop him. "Maximus, please be careful . . ."

"Careful? The Emperor was murdered!" said Maximus.

"No," said Quintus. "The Emperor died in his sleep."

Maximus looked toward the entrance of the tent and saw four royal guards with their swords ready. They came in and quickly tied his hands and arms.

"Please don't fight, Maximus," said Quintus. "I'm sorry . . . Caesar has spoken."

Maximus understood. Quintus was a soldier, and his orders had come from the top. He had to obey.

"Quintus ... promise me you'll look after my family," said Maximus.

"Your family will greet you in the next world," Quintus said, quietly.

Maximus jumped at him in anger. One of the guards hit the prisoner on the back of the head with the handle of his sword and Maximus fell to the ground.

"Take him as far as the sunrise and then kill him," said Quintus.

♦

It was nearly sunrise, and the five horses on the forest road had not passed anybody for several hours. Here there was nothing— no help, no hope.

"All right, this is far enough," said Cornelius, the oldest of the guards and their leader. "Take him down there. No one will ever find him."

Two of the guards climbed from their horses and pulled Maximus from his horse. His hands were still tied in front of him.

Cornelius searched in his bag for something to eat. He would make sure the orders from Caesar were obeyed but he did not want to have Roman blood on his hands. The other man, Salvius, stayed with the three horses.

The two guards led Maximus down the hill. They thought he had given up the fight, but he was like a cat watching a mouse. He could see they were young and their armor was still new. These were royal guards—they almost never left Rome and they did not usually go into battle. They were not experienced fighters.

"This is good enough," said one of them. "On your knees."

Behind Maximus, one of the guards was ready with his sword to cut off his head. The second guard stood facing Maximus.

Maximus sunk to his knees and closed his eyes. As the sword came down, he turned very quickly and caught it between his hands. Then he brought the handle of the sword up into the guard's face. In the next second he turned again and struck the sword through the other guard. As he got to his feet and turned back to the first man, he saw his chance and pushed the sword through his body.

On the road above, Cornelius and Salvius were waiting on their horses. They heard a cry from below, and then it was quiet again. Cornelius sent Salvius down to make certain Maximus was dead. The guard rode down the hill but saw nothing of his friends. Suddenly, he felt there was someone behind him. He turned in time to see Maximus's sword as it flew through the air toward him and landed in his chest. He fell to his death.

Cornelius was still on his horse, eating his bread and meat. He heard some noises below, moved across the road, and looked down into the trees. With no sound at all Maximus came onto the road behind him.

"Guard!" he shouted.

Cornelius turned around and rode toward Maximus at full speed, his sword ready. As they met, Maximus struck his sword upward and back. It cut right through Cornelius's body. Cornelius fell off his horse and lay down to die.

But Maximus had also been wounded, with a deep cut to his shoulder from Cornelius's sword. He fought the pain and moved toward the horses.

Chapter 4   A Prisoner Again

Maximus rode fast through the German forests on Cornelius's horse. He was leading one of the other horses behind him. He had put a cloth around the cut in his shoulder, but it was bad and gave him a lot of pain. Blood ran down his arm as he rode, but he did not have time to stop.

By the middle of the day he had crossed into the east of France. He rode his horse as hard as he could—he had to get home before it was too late.

Into the night he continued riding, not stopping for water, food, or rest. He saw nothing as he passed through the country and he remembered nothing. He could only think that time was passing so quickly. He became hot and tired and decided to throw off his armor. His horse was also tired, and he knew it could not go much further. He changed horses and continued his urgent flight toward Spain and the faraway hills above Trujillo.

◆

In the light of early day, the Spanish hills around the farm and house were unbelievably beautiful.

An eight-year-old boy with dark hair was in a field beside the pink stone house. He was training a wild horse, making it walk around the field. A beautiful, black-haired woman watched her son working with the horse and smiled. He would have a fine riding horse by the time his father returned.

The boy stopped—he saw something. Over a hill he could just see a battle flag, coming in their direction. He shouted with excitement and happiness and ran out of the field. He ran toward the flag, calling, "Father! Father!"

The woman, too, looked toward the flag. But there was something about it that worried her. Something was not right, and she suddenly felt anxious.

The boy continued to run along the road. Soon soldiers appeared over the hill. But they were not the Roman soldiers he expected to see. He slowed down, then stopped, confused. Twenty royal guards were riding down the road, and his father was not among them. He searched their faces again, looking for his father, hoping.

Behind him his mother started shouting out his name. The horses suddenly came faster, riding over the small boy and crashing him into the dirt of the road. Then they rode straight toward his screaming mother.

◆

As the hills turned pink and gold with the sunset, a rider raced for his life, killing the horse under him. His shoulder was bleeding badly. He came to the top of a long, low hill and stopped. There was a line of thick, black smoke in the distance and he tried to see where it was coming from. With a cry of pain he forced the horse forward, racing down the far side of the hill. Would he arrive in time?

Maximus's worst dream did not equal the sight in front of him. His family home and farm were burning, completely destroyed. The wheat and the apple trees were burnt black, and smoke still curved upward from the last stones of his house. Two pink stone chimneys were left standing—nothing else.

He stopped the horse violently. It fell over onto its side and Maximus was thrown off. His stomach was sick with fear. He knew now what he would find.

He stopped before the field of vegetables, looked up, and forced himself to breathe. There, hanging on ropes, were the burnt bodies of his wife and son. There was almost nothing left of them. He reached up with both hands to touch his wife's feet. A terrible scream came from him, and he sank to the earth. His world was now dead.

◆

Maximus dug one deep hole in the black earth on the hillside for his wife and son. He pushed the earth back over their broken, burnt bodies and cried. He looked down toward the ruin of the house he had built, to the dead apple trees.

He spoke to his loved ones through his tears. "Lie in the shadow of the trees, my loves, and wait for me there . . ."

He fell onto the earth beside them.

♦

They came because they had smelled the smoke in the air. Fire meant there was something to be found and taken.

These were Spanish thieves, and their chief was a big mountain man with a black beard. They found the man lying dead on the black earth. Hands touched his shoes—expensive, leather shoes. Other hands moved over his soldier's clothes—fine, dark red cloth.

Suddenly, the dead man moved. The hands on his body stopped. Something was said in a strange language. Everyone waited.

The big man on the ground did not move again. The chief made a sign to his men, and the hands roughly took hold of Maximus and pulled him away.

Days and nights passed, and for Maximus it was like a never-ending feverish dream. Terrible pictures crossed his mind as he lay close to death in the open carriage they had thrown him into. He dreamed of wild animals, close to his face . . . then he was on a ship, traveling across water. A large African man smiled down at him . . . he saw views of the desert . . . far-away mountains . . . heard shouts in a strange language. It was hot, too hot to breathe . . .

Maximus's eyes opened slowly. Centimeters away from his face was a wild tiger—and this one did not go away when he closed his eyes and opened them again.

He looked around and realized that he was one of several men chained together in a dirty slave carriage. There were small windows at the front and back and on both sides. He looked through one of the windows and saw other carriages traveling with them. Wild animals in chains were walking along with them, some close to the window that he was looking through. He fell back onto the floor, thinking, "This must all be a terrible dream."

When Maximus woke again, he saw twelve slaves, all chained together, all looking at him. Outside the carriage he could hear men talking in a language he did not understand. Someone was looking down at him, a big African man.

"Juba," said the African, giving his name. He, too, was chained.

Maximus moved with great pain and saw that the sword wound on his shoulder was worse than he had realized. Juba was putting something on the wound. Maximus fell back again and slept.

When he woke again, the African was still with him. "You see?" he said. "Now your arm is getting better—it's clean." He put his finger gently on the wound. "Don't die," said Juba. "They'll feed you to the tigers. They're more expensive than we are."

Maximus stared at him, and Juba looked down with a small smile on his lips.

♦

The desert heat of Morocco was not like anything that Maximus had known. The hot air made breathing difficult. He did not care about breathing, though. Maximus did not care about anything.

All around him men were standing in the sand in a slave market. The buyers walked slowly around, looking at the men and touching them. There was a man with a black beard standing near them, calling out to tell people about his slaves.

Maximus stood with the others, looking far away, beyond the people and the market. Physically, he was getting better with Juba's help. But nobody could help the darkness inside him. He did not even care about his own life. Maximus the Roman

General, Maximus the farmer and husband was already dead.

Across the market square Aelius Proximo sat in a small, dirty café and watched everything with interest. Proximo was a large man with big, blue eyes and white hair and beard. He looked like a man who enjoyed the good things in life. He drank his tea slowly, as a man measured his feet for new shoes. Two slave girls sat beside him.

"Proximo, my friend!" said the man with the black beard. Proximo recognized the man immediately and turned away. "Every day you are here is a great day," the man said, smiling. He came to sit with Proximo. "And today is your lucky day."

Proximo caught hold of his arm and held it tight. "It wasn't my lucky day the last time you sold me some animals. They're no good—they only run around and eat. Give me my money back!"

The slave-seller tried to pull his arm away. "I'll give you a special price today—because you are unhappy. Just for you. Come and see the new tigers."

Proximo let him go and followed him across the square.

"Look at this one," said the man. "Isn't he a beauty?"

Proximo looked at the tigers through the bars. "Do they fight?" he asked.

"Of course! For you, my special price, only eight thousand."

"For me," said Proximo, "four thousand. That's my special price."

"Four? I have to eat . . ."

Proximo looked around at the group of men in chains. "Do any of them fight?" he said. "There's a contest soon."

"Some are good for fighting, some for dying. You need both."

Proximo walked over to Juba. "Get up," he commanded the big African.

Juba lifted his head and looked at him. He got up slowly. Proximo looked at him carefully. He turned over Juba's hands and felt the hard skin.

Then he moved on to Maximus. He saw the wound on his

arm and then he saw the mark just above it—the letters "SPQR." Proximo knew that they meant *Senatus Populusque Romanus*: The Senate and the Roman People.

"A soldier," said Proximo. "Did you run away?" he asked Maximus. But Maximus said nothing.

"Probably," said the slave-seller. "They say he's a Spaniard."

Proximo walked on and looked at the others. "I'll take six—a thousand for all of them," he said. His servant handed him a small brush with red paint on it.

"A thousand!" the slave-seller cried. "The African alone should cost two thousand." He whispered to Proximo, "Turn your back on him, he'll kill you."

"These slaves are no good," said Proximo, as he walked away.

"Wait, wait . . . we can discuss the price."

Proximo made a mark in red paint on the chests of the slaves he had chosen. "I'll give you two thousand," he said, "and four for the animals. But it will be five thousand for an old friend."

The slave-seller thought for a second and then accepted.

"But those tigers have to fight," said Proximo.

"Don't feed them for a day and a half," said the slave-seller, "and they'll eat their own mothers."

"Interesting idea," said Proximo, as he walked away.

His servants pulled the chains tied to Juba, Maximus, and the others, and they were led away.

◆

Proximo's carriages arrived in a crowded, Moroccan port city. Maximus and Juba sat together with twelve other new slaves. One was a small, very frightened Greek man. He was probably a teacher or a writer. He was definitely not a fighter.

The carriage of slaves was followed by several others carrying wild animals—including the tigers. Most of the chained men looked back at the tigers from time to time, not with interest but with fear. They knew what a hungry tiger could do, and they guessed why they and the animals had been bought together.

They drove through some large iron gates. There was no sign on the gates or on the buildings inside, but everyone in the city knew the place as Proximo's School. It was not a place to learn Latin, Greek, or mathematics. It was a school where men learned how to fight—to live one more day in the face of death. It was a gladiator school.

Proximo's school was like a castle prison. In the center was a square. On one side were the cages for the animals, and on the opposite side the human prisoners were kept.

Maximus and the other new slaves were pushed into their prison, and the doors crashed shut behind them. Maximus noticed the guards. They all carried short swords and some also had arrows or spears.

At the far end of the square a group of about ten men were training. "Battle practice," thought Maximus. "Like Commodus."

A very big man was teaching two new gladiators how to throw a spear. They were trying to hit a picture of a man, but they were not very good. Both students missed it. The teacher threw his spear and hit the picture in the stomach.

"Haken," said a voice from behind, naming the teacher.

Maximus turned to see Proximo, who was admiring Haken's strength. He and Maximus stared at each other.

"Spaniard ..." Proximo said, naming Maximus. Then he moved along the line, naming each new slave. "Thief ... murderer ..."

Suddenly, he stopped and smiled. "Proximo!" he said. "Anyone know the meaning of that? 'Nearest.' 'Dearest.' 'Close to.' I am Proximo. I shall be closer to you in the next days than your own mothers were. I did not pay good money to buy you," Proximo said. "I paid to buy your *death*. You may die alone, in pairs, or in groups—who knows? Many different ways with just one ending." He walked around his new slaves, enjoying himself. "And when you die—and you will die—the sound of cheering will send you to the next world."

Proximo raised his hands and stretched them out to the group of slaves. "Gladiators, I salute you," he said.

Chapter 5   New Gladiators

Proximo never missed training for the new boys. He could learn so much about them.

The more experienced gladiators trained against each other, working with swords and spears and with shields and armor.

The new ones were put together into a small arena in the center. One by one they were given heavy wooden swords and sent in to face the teacher. He had a similar sword.

Proximo watched from a short distance. Very quickly his trained eye could sort the new class into two groups. The fighters were marked with red paint, and the others with yellow.

Haken enjoyed his job as gladiator teacher. He took great pleasure in knocking away the swords of his new students and then hitting them hard so they fell onto the dirt. It was soon Maximus's turn to face Haken.

"Spaniard," Haken called to him.

Maximus went forward slowly. Proximo watched more closely, to see what would happen.

Maximus picked up the sword and stood facing Haken. Suddenly everyone, especially Haken, saw that this man was a fighter. There was something about the way he held the sword, the way he stood—but most of all there were his eyes. There was no doubt—he knew how to fight.

Maximus lifted the sword and then dropped it to the ground. He seemed to be saying, "I could kill, but I choose not to."

Haken was surprised. Was this an insult? He looked to Proximo for orders. Proximo made a sign to him to continue.

Haken struck Maximus across the stomach. Maximus fell forward but then stood straight again and faced him.

Haken looked again to Proximo, and again he was told to continue.

This time Haken struck Maximus across his wounded arm. Maximus almost fell to the ground but managed to stay on his feet. All the time he stared straight at Haken, who was becoming very angry. Maximus's thoughts were clear: "I may be low, but I'm not as low as you. I won't kill for sport."

Proximo found it very interesting. Haken lifted the sword again, ready to hurt Maximus really badly, but Proximo stopped him. "That's enough for now," he said. "His time will come." He looked behind him to the servant with the pots of paint. "Mark that one," he said.

♦

In the heat of the late afternoon Haken, Juba, the Greek, and the other new gladiators sat on the ground in the shadows.

Maximus lay by the wall to one side. He had a small, sharp stone and was using it to try to remove the letters SPQR from his arm.

Juba called out to him, "Spaniard! Why didn't you fight? We all have to fight."

Maximus did not answer.

The young Greek was very frightened. "I don't fight," he said. "I shouldn't be here. I'm a secretary—I can write in seven languages."

"Good," said Haken. "Tomorrow you can scream in seven languages."

The other gladiators laughed.

Juba moved closer to Maximus and watched him digging the stone into his skin. "Is that the sign of your gods?" he asked.

Maximus did not answer.

Behind them Haken was making fun of the Greek. "Maybe the secretary will be the one who wins his freedom," he laughed.

"Freedom!" the Greek replied. "What do I have to do?"

"You go into the arena and you kill me," Haken replied. "Then you kill him, and the African, and him, and a hundred more. And when there are no more men to fight, you're free."

"I can't do that," cried the Greek.

"No," said Haken, suddenly serious, "but I can." He looked from one gladiator to the next until his eyes rested on Maximus.

Maximus stared back at him, his face like stone.

◆

Proximo and his gladiators walked through the streets of the town on their way to the arena. Haken and the gladiators were chained together, and Proximo's guards walked with them. They were all carrying short swords.

The arena was small. It was not like the enormous Colosseum* in Rome, although it was there for the same reason—to entertain the people. This arena was just a circle of sandy ground with a lot of seats around it. But the seats were filled with people, and the people were expecting to see blood.

Maximus and the other gladiators were taken to a small area behind the seats. Above them were Proximo's seats, next to the seats of several other gladiator trainers. This special position gave the trainers a good view of the arena and they could also see the gladiators preparing to fight. They discussed their gladiators together before the contest started—who would live and who would die.

"Has the African fought before?" one of the men asked Proximo.

* Colosseum: the famous arena in Rome, used for gladiator contests.

"No, first time."

"And that one?" he asked, pointing to Maximus. "Soldier?"

"Him? He's no good," said Proximo. "But I have an idea." He called down to his guards. "Chain the Spaniard to the African," he said.

The other man was not sure about Maximus. He liked the look of the Spaniard. "I think he'll live through this fight, you think he'll die," he said. "Let's put money on the result—a thousand?"

"Against my own man? I don't do that," said Proximo.

"And if I make it five thousand?"

Proximo thought about it. That was a lot of money.

◆

Proximo liked to see his new boys before they went to fight. A guard called for silence as he walked into the waiting area.

"Some of you are thinking that you won't fight," Proximo said, "and some that you *can't* fight. They all say that until they're out there." He pulled a sword down from a shelf. "Push this into another man and the crowd will cheer and love you. You may even begin to love them back." He stuck the point of the sword in a table. "In the end, we are all dead men. Sadly, we cannot choose how. But we can decide how we accept that end, so we are remembered as men. You go out into the arena as slaves. You come back—if you come back—as gladiators."

Outside, the crowd was getting impatient. Before he left, Proximo walked down the line of men, saying who must be chained together. They were all put in teams of two—and it soon became clear that the method was to chain a "Red" to a "Yellow." Each good fighter was with a certain loser.

Haken was chained to the crying Greek secretary. Maximus— a "loser" because he had refused to fight Haken—was chained to Juba.

Maximus turned to look at the closed door. From the other side they could hear the shouts of the crowd. Suddenly, Maximus bent down and picked up a little sand from the ground, then let it fall through his fingers. Juba watched him but did not understand. When Maximus stood up again, he looked different. He was ready for battle.

Outside, the crowds were cheering and shouting. There was the sound of drums. Everyone stood anxiously waiting.

Suddenly, the doors to the arena crashed open and sunlight poured in. For a few seconds the men were blinded by it. There were trained gladiators already in the arena, waiting, their swords and spears ready for killing.

The new gladiators ran out, some to immediate death. Side by side, their chain loose between them, Maximus and Juba ran out into the arena.

It was not a fair fight. The new men had only one small sword and no armor; the experienced gladiators had much better equipment.

Maximus and Juba fought together. Juba was surprised to see that his partner—marked with the yellow of cowards—was fighting bravely. All the anger and pain inside Maximus had come out, and he was better than any man in the arena. He knew this was not his day to die, not like this.

Together they killed the first pair of gladiators. Others came to fight them and, for a second, Juba lost his sword as he attacked. Maximus pulled him clear of the other man's sword and then struck the attacker hard. His sword point came out the man's back. He and Juba worked together as a team. They were strong and fast, and many of the attacking gladiators were killed by them.

Haken fought with great power. The Greek was soon killed, and Haken cut off the man's hand so it was easier for him to move about in the arena.

Proximo watched everything closely.

The crowd quickly realized that Juba and Maximus were a strong fighting pair and began to cheer them.

Soon all the attackers were on the ground. Juba and Maximus looked around, and then at each other. But then, as they began to relax, one of the gladiators tried to get to his feet. They ran forward together and pulled their chain tightly around his neck.

The fighting had ended. The crowd were on their feet, cheering. Maximus looked at the many bodies around him, and then at the excited faces of the crowd. It made him sick that people were entertained by the sight of men killing other men. He walked toward the entrance and threw his sword into the crowd. It only made them cheer louder.

Proximo was pleased with the day's work. He had lost a lot of money but he had found a new fighter.

Chapter 6   Caesar's Arrival in Rome

It was a special day in Rome, a holiday. Fifty black-armored royal guards marched down the main street of Rome, followed by hundreds of men on horses. Behind them came the royal carriage. Commodus, the new Emperor of Rome, was coming home.

His sister Lucilla was sitting next to him. Another fifty guards marched behind them. Close to the royal carriage, on a beautiful black horse, rode Quintus, the new Commander of the Royal Guards.

Commodus had told the Senate that he was now the Commander of the Roman Army, and that the army was loyal to him. Many senators doubted it, but there was no one in Rome with enough power to take control. And so nothing could stop Commodus.

The people had been told that their new Emperor would arrive in Rome on this date, at this time. The city was cleaned up and purple flags were hung outside the most important buildings. The citizens of Rome lined the streets at the time he was expected.

The crowd was not very big and it was not very enthusiastic. They cheered, but not loudly. Commodus was young and had no experience, but the people could forgive that. They were more worried about the stories they had heard—that Commodus was selfish and cruel. He was not his father, and they had loved Marcus Aurelius. Commodus had much work to do to make himself popular and win the support of the people.

Ahead, on the steps of the Senate, a group of senators stood waiting: Falco, Gaius, and Gracchus were among them. Lucius, Lucilla's eight-year-old son, was standing with them.

Senator Gracchus, a white-haired man in his sixties, was not happy about the new Emperor. "He is entering Rome like a hero—but what has he ever done?" he said.

"Give him time, Gracchus," Falco answered. "He's young. I think he could do very well."

"For Rome?" asked Gracchus. "Or for you?"

Falco turned to Lucius. "It's a proud day for all of us, isn't it, Lucius?" he said. "I'm sure Senator Gracchus never thought he'd live to see such a day."

Lucius watched as the royal carriage came closer, then ran down the steps when it arrived. He jumped up into his mother's arms and she held him tight and kissed him.

Commodus raised his arm in salute to the crowd, but he could see that the crowd was small and the cheering was only polite.

"Rome greets her new Emperor," Falco said. "Your loyal people are here to welcome you, sir."

"Thank you, Falco," replied Commodus, "for bringing out the loyal people. I hope they weren't too expensive." He turned to Gracchus. "Ah, Gracchus," he said. "The friend of Rome."

"We are happy that you are home, Caesar," Gracchus said.

Then he became more serious. "There are many problems that need your attention."

◆

In the royal palace Commodus was meeting with the senators. He was following his sister's advice and listening to them patiently.

Senator Gracchus had a list of problems in the city. He was anxious that Commodus look at them without delay. ". . . and here are some suggestions from the Senate—ideas for solving the problems," he said.

Commodus walked around the room, losing interest. Lucilla listened carefully—and watched her brother.

Finally, Commodus could not listen any longer. "You see Gracchus, this is exactly the problem," he interrupted. "My father spent too much time listening to the Senate, and the people were forgotten."

"The Senate *is* the people, Caesar," said Gracchus. "Chosen from among the people, to speak for the people."

"I doubt many of the people eat as well as you do, Gracchus. Or have the beautiful home you have, Gaius. I think I understand my own people," Commodus said.

"Would Caesar kindly teach us, from his own great experience?" replied Gracchus.

"I call it love, Gracchus. I am their father. The people are my children," said Commodus. He was getting angry.

Lucilla stepped forward. "Senators, my brother is very tired," she said. "Please leave your list with me. Caesar will do everything that Rome needs." She called for a slave to show them out.

The senators left, but they were not pleased. It was not a good start for the new Emperor. When they had gone, Lucilla turned to Commodus. "The Senate can be useful," she said.

"How?" he replied. "They only talk." He moved to a window

and looked out over the great city. "It should be just you, and me, and Rome."

"There has always been a Senate . . ." said Lucilla.

"Rome has changed," he answered. "It takes an emperor to rule an empire."

"Of course, but leave the people their traditions."

It had been a "tradition" for the last two hundred years to believe that the Senate ruled Rome, through the Emperor. But everyone knew the real situation. The army held the political power in Rome, and the real ruler was whoever the army was loyal to.

Commodus's thoughts were moving ahead. "All the years of my father's wars gave the people nothing—but still they loved him. Why? They didn't see the battles. They knew nothing of the people we fought and killed, or their countries," he said.

"They care about the greatness of Rome," said Lucilla.

"And what is that? Can I touch it, see it?"

"It's an idea. It's something they want to believe in," said Lucilla.

Commodus was suddenly excited. "I'll give them something to believe in—I'll give them great ideas. And they'll love me for it," he said, raising his arms to the sky. "I will give them the greatest ideas, the most wonderful Rome ever!"

◆

There were artists at work in the streets, painting enormous pictures on walls. Their pictures showed scenes of gladiators and wild animals fighting, and the sand on the floors of the arenas was red with blood. Crowds stood and stared, watching as the pictures were completed. This was the start of the advertising for Commodus's new idea.

"Games!" Gaius complained to Gracchus and a group of other senators as he joined them in a café. "One hundred and fifty days of games!"

The senators watched the wall painters working outside the café.

"He's smarter than I thought," said Gracchus, quietly.

"Smart?" said Gaius. "All of Rome would laugh at him if they weren't so afraid of his guards. You can't really think that the people will forget Rome's problems and sit back to enjoy these games?" he asked. "It's completely mad."

"I think he knows what Rome is," Gracchus replied. "He will give them magic, and then they'll have something else to think about. He will take their lives, and he will take their freedom. And still they will shout and cheer." He shook his head, sadly. "The beating heart of Rome isn't in the walls of the Senate. It's on the sand of the Colosseum. He will give them death. And they will love him for it."

The other senators knew he was right. It was a lesson from history. But they did not know that Commodus was planning better and longer games than any emperor before him. And it was all for one reason. Commodus knew he had no choice. He and the Senate did not agree about anything and he could not be certain of their support. So he had to look beyond the Senate and go straight to the people for his power. The games were the key. As Lucilla had said, the people must have their traditions. And he would not deny his citizens their traditional games.

Sitting behind the senators in the café, with his back to them, was a small man. None of the senators noticed him, but he was close enough to hear everything they said. The face of the listener was quite ordinary, except that his right eye was missing. He did not see well with only one eye, but he could hear perfectly and he had a good memory. He was able to collect a lot of information and he was paid well to repeat it to other ears.

Chapter 7 The Spaniard and the Crowd

Crowds of people came down the hillside from their small houses above the Moroccan town. They were all going toward the arena, hoping to put a little excitement into their difficult lives.

Maximus's arm, now without the letters SPQR, was covered with an arm guard. He had earned the extra protection of armor because of his brave fighting. He bent and picked up some dirt from the ground, watched it disappear through his fingers, and walked quickly toward the entrance to the arena. Proximo walked with him.

"You just kill, kill, kill!" Proximo shouted at Maximus. "You make it look too easy. The crowd wants a hero, not just someone cutting up meat. We want them to keep coming back. Don't kill so quickly—take more time!" The cheers of the crowd grew louder as they got closer to the arena. "Give them an adventure to remember!" Proximo shouted above the noise. "Fall to one knee—they'll think you're finished. Then force yourself to your feet—our hero!" He was rushing along to keep up with Maximus. "Remember, you're an entertainer!"

Without a word to Proximo, Maximus walked out into the arena. There was a cheer immediately. He was a known fighter now, and the Moroccans knew they were going to see some real action.

Out in the bright sunlight, six fighters waited. Maximus looked at them and decided immediately on his method of attack. He chose the strongest and most confident man first. When that man went down, the others would know they had no chance. He cut them down, one by one, his sword striking through their bodies with great speed. It was all finished in a few minutes.

The crowd stood and cheered. They shouted, "Spaniard! Spaniard!"

Proximo got up from his seat and walked out.

Maximus dropped his arm to his side, stepped over a body, and walked back toward the exit. He picked up a sword from the sand and threw it into the crowd. As it fell to the floor, the screaming crowd grew silent, watching and waiting.

"Are you not entertained?" Maximus shouted at them. "Is this not why you came?" He threw down his own sword and walked out of the arena gates and back to the prison area.

◆

In the cool of the evening, Maximus and Juba stood inside the gates of Proximo's school. They looked out over the desert to the mountains in the distance.

"My country—it's somewhere out there," Juba said. "My home. My wife is preparing food and my daughters are carrying water from the river. Will I ever see them again? I think not."

"Do you believe you'll meet them again—after you die?" Maximus asked.

"I think so," Juba said. "But I will die soon. They will not die for many years."

"But you would wait for them."

"Of course," Juba said.

"I almost died, coming here," said Maximus. "You saved me. I never thanked you." Maximus looked at Juba, and there was pain in his eyes. "Because my wife, and my son, are waiting for me."

Juba understood. "You'll meet them again," he said. "But not yet, yes?" He laughed. This team was not ready for death.

Later that evening, two guards came to find Maximus. They took him to Proximo.

"Ah, Spaniard," he said, sending the guards away. "It worries me that although you're good, you could be better. You could be the greatest."

"You want me to kill. I kill," Maximus said. "That's enough." He turned to walk out.

"Enough for a small Moroccan town like this," Proximo called after him. "But not for Rome."

Maximus stopped. "Rome?" he said, suddenly interested.

"My men have just brought the news," Proximo said. "The young Emperor has arranged some games in honor of his dead father, Marcus Aurelius. It's strange to think that I had to leave my school in Rome years ago because his father stopped all gladiator contests. But his day has ended now."

"Yes," said Maximus, quietly, angrily.

Proximo laughed. "We're going back! After five years in this terrible place we're going back to the Colosseum," he said. "Ah, Spaniard, wait until you fight in the Colosseum. Fifty thousand Romans following every move of your sword. The silence before you strike. The cry that comes after—like a storm!" He stopped and looked to the heavens, his eyes shining.

Maximus saw the memories lighting up Proximo's face and suddenly he understood. "You were once a gladiator," he said.

Proximo looked back at him. "The best," he said.

"You won your freedom?" Maximus asked.

"A long time ago." Proximo went into the next room and came back carrying a small wooden sword. "The Emperor gave me this. A sign of freedom. He touched me on the shoulder and I was free."

On the handle of the sword was Proximo's name and the words, "Free man—By Order of the Emperor Marcus Aurelius."

"I, too, want to stand in front of the Emperor, as you did."

"Then listen to me," said Proximo. "Learn from me. I was not the best because I killed quickly. I was the best because the crowd loved me. Win the crowd, and you'll win your freedom."

Maximus knew that he was right. "I'll win the crowd. I'll give them something they've never seen before."

◆

In the royal palace Commodus stood looking down at Lucius, asleep in his bed. Lucilla entered quietly behind him. She stood in the doorway, watching, worried.

"He sleeps so well because he is loved," said Commodus, gently brushing a hair from Lucius's face.

Lucilla moved forward quickly. Lucius turned over and she thought he was waking. "Shh . . . go back to sleep now," she said. She pulled his blanket closer and watched him breathe deeply, already dreaming again. "Come, brother, it's late," she said, turning away and knowing he would follow her.

Back in his own room Commodus sat on the bed and picked up a document. He looked at it, then let it fall to the floor. The table next to his bed was covered in other papers—plans for the New Rome and documents from the Senate.

"I can't sleep," he complained. "The Senate is always sending me papers. And my own dreams for Rome are making my head ache."

Lucilla prepared a drink for him, secretly mixing in some medicine. "Quiet, brother, this will help." She held out the drink to him and watched as he drank it.

"Are the people ready for me to close the Senate yet? What do you think? Should I have the senators killed? Some or all of them?" he asked Lucilla.

"We'll talk about it tomorrow. Sleep now," she said. She thought to herself, "Rome is in frightening hands. Thank the gods that I am here to control him."

"Will you stay with me?" Commodus asked Lucilla.

"Still afraid of the dark, brother?" Lucilla smiled gently, kissed him, and then started to go. She stopped at the door and looked back.

Commodus lay on the bed, a lonely figure, his eyes wide open.

"Sleep, brother," Lucilla said.

"You know my dreams would bring terror to the world," he said.

Lucilla left.

♦

When she was certain that Commodus was asleep, Lucilla quietly left the palace. She went to Senator Gracchus's house, and there in the darkness Gaius was waiting for her. He took her arm and led her into the house, where Gracchus met them in the hall.

He turned to Lucilla. "Do you know, there was a time, not very long ago, when I held two children on my knee," he said with a kind smile. "They were the most beautiful children I'd ever seen. And their father was very proud of them. I, too, loved them very much, like my own."

"And they loved you," said Lucilla.

"I saw one of them grow strong and good," Gracchus continued. "The other grew ... dark. I watched as his father turned away from him. We all turned away from him. And as he became more and more lonely, there was more hate than love in his heart." Gracchus shook his head sadly.

They went into the main room and Gracchus gave his guests glasses of wine. Lucilla spoke first. "Anyone who says anything against the Emperor is in danger now," she said. "Students, teachers, writers ... we must be careful."

"All to feed the arena. I'm afraid to go out after dark," said Gaius.

"You should be more afraid in the day," said Gracchus. "The Senate is full of Falco's spies." He took a glass of wine and sat next to Lucilla. "What is in Commodus's mind? These games are all he seems to care about."

"And how is he paying for them?" asked Gaius. "They must cost a fortune each day, but we have no new taxes."

41

"The future is paying," Lucilla answered. "He's started selling the wheat we have saved. In two years time the people will die of hunger. I hope they're enjoying the games now because soon these games will be the reason their children are dead."

"This can't be true," said Gaius. "Rome must know this."

"And who will tell them?" asked Lucilla. "You, Gaius? Or you, Gracchus? Will you make a speech in the Senate and then see your family killed in the Colosseum?" She looked from one man to the other. "He must die," she said.

"Quintus and the guards would take control themselves," said Gaius.

"And we haven't got enough men. The army may not be loyal to us," said Gracchus. "No, we must wait, prepare, and be ready. We can do nothing while he has the support of the people. But every day he makes more enemies. One day he will have more enemies than friends, and then we will strike. Until then, we must be patient."

◆

Proximo and his gladiators were near Rome by late afternoon. Proximo could see that something had changed since he left five years before. Rome had become an army camp.

When they were inside the city walls, he noticed other things. The city was poorer and dirtier than he remembered it.

At last they arrived at Proximo's old school, where the gates were still locked as he had left them. The gladiators were glad to get out of the box they had traveled in. They looked around. Across the rooftops of Rome, only a short distance away, was an enormous building: the great Colosseum.

Maximus, Juba, and the others stared at it, listening to the sound of 50,000 voices shouting for blood. Each man was thinking, "Is that where I die?"

From the great arena came another sound: "Caesar! Caesar!"

42

Proximo knew this meant that the Emperor had just arrived. He looked across at Maximus. "Win the crowd," he said softly.

Maximus had only one thought: "He is there. He is close. The time is coming when I will see him myself: the man I live to kill."

♦

It was late morning of the following day when Maximus and the other gladiators were taken to the Colosseum. They were put into cages under the seats of the arena.

Crowds of people came past to look at the new fighters, to guess which ones were winners and which would die. Maximus sat at the back of the cage, taking no notice of them.

He could hear Proximo talking loudly to a man called Cassius, whose job was to organize the contests in the Colosseum. He also had to please the Emperor.

"The Emperor wants battles?" Proximo shouted. "My men are highly trained single fighters. I refuse to let them die like that. They will be wasted in this stupid piece of theater."

"The crowd wants battles, so the Emperor gives them battles," Cassius replied, "and your gladiators are going to act the Battle of Carthage★. You have no choice."

Their voices grew quieter as they walked away.

Among the passing crowds were some young boys from rich families, watched by their servants. Maximus took no notice of them until a voice suddenly made him turn his head.

"Gladiator!" It was one of the boys, fair-haired and about the same age as Maximus's son. "Gladiator, are you the one they call 'the Spaniard?'" he asked.

Maximus moved closer to the boy. "Yes," he said.

"They said you were enormous. They said you could squeeze a man's head until it broke, with just one hand," said the boy.

★ Battle of Carthage: the last of a number of wars between Rome and the city of Carthage (now Tunis) in North Africa in 146 B.C. (before the birth of Christ).

43

Maximus looked down at his hand. "A man's? No ..." he said. He held out his hand and smiled. "But maybe a boy's ..."

The boy smiled back. "I like you, Spaniard," he said. "I shall cheer for you."

Maximus was shocked. "They let you watch the games?" he asked.

"My uncle says they will make me strong," the boy replied.

"But what does your father say?"

"My father's dead."

The boy's servant came to him and took his hand. "Come, Lucius. It's time to go."

"Your name's Lucius?" asked Maximus.

"Lucius Verus, like my father," Lucius said proudly. He turned and left, followed by the servant.

With a shock, Maximus suddenly realized that the boy must be Lucilla's son. He searched the crowd—was Lucilla somewhere out there? But although he kept looking, he could not see her. He could only see the faces of people who were thirsty for blood.

Chapter 8   The Colosseum

The gladiators waited for their contest in an area that was at the same level as the sand of the arena. In there they were given helmets, body armor, and swords.

Proximo's guards led his gladiators into the area and Maximus walked over to a window. He looked out at the sand that seemed to continue for ever.

Maximus spoke in a low voice to one of the guards. "Is the Emperor here?" he asked.

"He'll be here," the guard replied. "He comes every day."

One of the guards held out a helmet to Maximus. He shook his head and looked instead at the other helmets. He chose one with a better face guard and tried it on. He turned his head back toward the arena, knowing that now his face could not be recognized.

Proximo's gladiators were armored and ready. They were dressed to look like soldiers from Carthage. They carried spears and long, curved, heavy shields.

As they waited to go out into the arena, an official spoke to them. "You have the honor of fighting in front of the Emperor himself," he said. "When the Emperor enters, raise your spears in salute. When you salute him, speak together," he said. "Face the Emperor. Don't turn your backs."

"Go," Proximo said. "Die with honor." His five best gladiators walked past him and onto the sand of the arena.

Maximus was the last to step onto the floor of the great Colosseum. He had never imagined such a sight. There were thousands and thousands of screaming, shouting people. All around him was an ocean of cheering faces. It took his breath away.

The gladiators moved into the center of the sand. At the same time, three other teams appeared in the arena from different entrances. There was now a total of twenty gladiators on the Colosseum stage. All wore the same armor and carried long double-pointed spears and heavy metal shields. They stood in a line and faced the Emperor's seat. It was still empty. Fifty royal guards surrounded the area where Commodus and his friends would sit.

Then Commodus and Lucilla entered—and the crowd went wild, cheering and shouting salutes. Lucilla and Lucius went to their seats. Commodus moved forward and waved to the crowd.

Gaius and other senators near the Emperor watched in silence. They had just heard the latest news: To help pay for the games, Commodus was taking the houses and money of senators he disliked.

Commodus looked down at the gladiators, and Maximus froze as he felt his eyes rest on him. He stared up at the man he hated and wanted to kill. On one side of Commodus he saw Quintus.

45

On the other side, Lucilla and Lucius. The distance between them was too great—this was not his chance. He knew there would be a better one.

When Cassius gave a sign, the gladiators all saluted with their spears and shouted, "Caesar—we salute you before we die!" Only Maximus was silent.

Cassius stepped forward to introduce the afternoon's event. "On this day we reach back into history to bring you the Battle of Carthage!" The crowd cheered loudly. They laughed at the gladiators, dressed as the soldiers of Carthage, the battle's losers. Then Cassius continued, "On that great day the gods sent them against Rome's greatest soldiers—the Army of Africa!"

The crowd cheered again as the doors at the ends of the arena suddenly opened with a crash, and six chariots came in from each end. The chariots raced through the line of gladiators, who jumped out of the way. They turned and came back, running over one gladiator. Then the chariots raced around the outside of the arena, forcing the gladiators back into the center. It was difficult for the men on foot to see well through the cloud of dust and sand from the wheels of the chariots. As they thundered past, Maximus saw a spear flying through the air. It hit one of the gladiators in the neck and killed him immediately.

Maximus could see that he must take control and he called to the other gladiators, "If we work together, we can win!" He made them move in closer. "Shields together! Shoulders against the shields!" he called. The gladiators followed his orders—except for one. Haken stood alone, ready to fight his own battle.

The crowd was very surprised. They had never seen anything like this before! The men in the chariots circled around the group firing arrows and spears, but they only hit the gladiators' shields.

A Roman spear from one chariot hit Haken in the leg. Juba threw his spear and killed the driver, and Maximus pulled Haken into the safety of the group.

Two chariots drove straight at the gladiators. Fixed to their wheels were short, sharp spears. As the wheels turned, they could cut a man to pieces. But the shields were good protection, and the wheel spears broke when they hit them. The wheel of one chariot hit the corner of a shield, and the chariot turned over. Another driver, close behind, crashed into it and was thrown out. His chariot raced on, and its wheel spears killed him as he tried to get away. A third chariot was very close, and both vehicles crashed into the gate.

Maximus ran for one of the broken chariots and cut the horse free. He jumped onto the horse and rode fast toward one chariot. The driver was watching Maximus carefully. He did not see that he was very close to another vehicle. Their wheels touched. Both drivers were thrown onto the sand. One was killed by Maximus's spear, and the other died under the feet of his horse.

The gladiators pulled two crashed chariots into the path of the others, who were forced to slow down. Then they rushed at the drivers, striking them with their spears.

Maximus looked around. All their enemies were dead. He climbed down from his horse, and the gladiators stood on either side of him. Haken was among them.

In the arena, Maximus, for the first time, raised his right arm and sword high. It was the gladiators' traditional sign of beating death. The crowd cheered wildly.

♦

Commodus called for Cassius.

"My history is not so good," he said, "but I thought we won the Battle of Carthage."

"Yes, sir," said Cassius, his voice shaking with fear. "Forgive me."

"Oh, I'm not unhappy," said Commodus. "I enjoy surprises." He pointed to Maximus. "Who is he?"

"They call him the Spaniard, sir."

"I think I'll meet him," said Commodus.

The gladiators were almost at the gate. Maximus turned and saw the Emperor walking out onto the sand, smiling at him. He noticed a broken arrow in the sand and, as he fell to his knees, he quickly closed his hand around it. This would be his chance.

Commodus was nearly there . . . just a little further . . . almost close enough to kill. Maximus was ready . . .

Suddenly, Lucius ran out and took Commodus by the hand. Commodus laughed and moved the boy in front of him, facing the gladiator hero. Maximus could not strike—Lucius was in the way.

"Stand, stand," said Commodus to Maximus. "Now, why doesn't the hero tell us his real name?" Maximus stood and said nothing. "You do have a name?" asked Commodus.

"My name is Gladiator," Maximus said. Then he turned and walked away. It was a great insult to turn his back on the Emperor. The crowd were shocked. Commodus was very angry.

He made a sign to Quintus, who moved the royal guards into the arena. They stood at the gate, swords ready, and did not let Maximus pass.

Commodus spoke calmly and clearly. "Slave," he said, "you will remove your helmet and tell me your name."

Slowly, Maximus turned to face him. He knew he had no choice now. He took off his helmet.

Commodus stared. Quintus could not believe his eyes. Lucilla recognized Maximus from her seat in the arena and put her hand over her mouth in total shock.

Maximus spoke in a clear, proud voice. "My name is Maximus Decimus Meridas, Commander of the Army of the North, General of the Western Armies, loyal servant to the true Emperor, Marcus Aurelius." The Colosseum was completely silent. Then he turned to Commodus and spoke more quietly. "I am father to a murdered son, husband to a murdered wife, and I will punish their killer, in this life or the next."

Commodus gave a sign to his guards and they moved closer.

The crowd shouted out. They had seen enough deaths for one afternoon and they did not want their hero to be the next one. They reached out a forest of thumbs, pointing up to the heavens. Their meaning was clear—Let him live!

Commodus looked around at his people and with great difficulty he forced himself to smile. He slowly lifted his own thumb.

The crowd cheered. "Maximus! Maximus!" they shouted.

Lucilla and the senators could not believe the scene happening in front of them.

Another shocked face was watching from his seat in the Colosseum. It was Cicero, Maximus's servant in the army. As he watched the General, his mind saw many possibilities.

Maximus led his men from the arena. He looked back just once, from the gate, and thought, "The battle hasn't ended yet."

♦

In the darkness of the palace Lucilla stopped in front of the doors to Commodus's room. She took a deep breath before she entered.

Commodus sat calmly at his desk, signing papers. Lucilla was surprised that he was not still in a violent temper. When he returned from the Colosseum, he had screamed in anger and attacked a picture of Marcus Aurelius. Now he was quieter and behaving quite normally. She walked up to the desk.

"Why is he still alive?" he asked her.

"I don't know," she said.

"He shouldn't be alive," her brother said. "That makes me angry. I am terribly angry."

Lucilla watched him carefully, waiting for an explosion.

"I only did the things I had to do," said Commodus. "Father's plan was crazy—the Empire ... Rome ... they must continue. You do understand that, don't you?"

"Yes," replied Lucilla.

He moved to the tall window and looked out at Rome, quiet now in the late night. "They lied to me in Germany. They told me he was dead. If they lie to me, they don't honor me. If they don't honor me, how can they ever love me?"

♦

Maximus was lying awake in the dark of the prison when he heard a guard coming. He was on his feet immediately.

The guard entered and took Maximus along to another prison room. He chained him to the wall and left without a word.

And into the light stepped a woman. Lucilla.

Maximus stared at her. "I knew your brother would send one of his killers," he said. "I didn't think he would send his best."

"Maximus, he doesn't know . . ." Lucilla began.

"My family were burnt alive!" Maximus interrupted, throwing the words at her in anger.

"I knew nothing of that, you must believe me. I cried for them."

"As you cried for your father?" said Maximus.

"I have been living in a prison of fear since that day," Lucilla said. "I live in terror for my son because he will be the next emperor . . ."

"My son was innocent," said Maximus.

"So is mine," she replied. "Must my son die, too, before you'll trust me?"

Maximus began then to relax. "Why does it matter if I trust you or not?" he asked.

"The gods have allowed you to live. Today I saw a slave become more powerful than the Emperor of Rome," she said. "Use that power, Maximus. My brother has many enemies, but until today no one was strong enough to face him. The people were with you, they would follow you."

"I am only one man. What possible difference can I make?"

"Some politicians have worked all their lives for the good of

Rome—one man above all. If I can arrange it, will you meet him?" she asked.

"Don't you understand? I could be killed tonight in this prison—or tomorrow in the arena. I'm just a slave now."

"This man wants the same things as you," said Lucilla.

"Then let *him* kill Commodus!" Maximus said in anger.

Lucilla searched for a way to make him understand. "I knew a man once," she said. "He loved my father very much and my father loved him. This man served Rome well."

"That man is gone," said Maximus. "Your brother did his work well."

"Let me help you," said Lucilla.

"Yes, you can help me. Forget you ever knew me," Maximus replied. "And never come here again." He shouted for the guard. "This lady has finished with me," he said.

The guard unlocked the door and led Maximus away.

Chapter 9   A Man for the People

Senator Gracchus climbed the many stairs inside the Colosseum. He listened to the shouting crowd and he was not enthusiastic about being there.

He joined a group of other senators near the top of the arena.

"Senator Gracchus," Falco said with surprise. "We don't often see you enjoying the pleasures of the crowd."

"I don't pretend to be a man of the people," said Gracchus. "But I do try to be a man *for* the people."

The Colosseum was full. The crowd was already beginning to shout the name of their hero and favorite gladiator. "Maximus . . . Maximus . . . Maximus."

Cassius started to introduce the next event of the day.

"Now, as we celebrate the sixty-fourth day of the games, you will see how kind the Emperor is and how he loves his people!"

Servants came into the arena pulling great boxes. They removed the covers and took out loaves of bread. Then they started to throw them into the crowd. Other servants appeared at the top of the steps and threw the bread down. There were thousands of loaves. The crowd cheered and caught as many loaves as they could.

Commodus chose this as the best time for him to enter.

Below, in the prison area, Proximo stood with Maximus. They heard a great cheer go up from the crowd.

"He certainly knows how to please them," said Proximo.

"Marcus Aurelius had a dream for Rome, Proximo," said Maximus. "This is not it."

"Marcus Aurelius is dead, Maximus," Proximo reminded him.

In the arena the servants had thrown all the bread to the crowd, and Cassius spoke again. "The Emperor has decided there will be a special contest today. Five years after his last fight in the Colosseum, we bring you the greatest gladiator in Roman history! Today Tigris of France returns!"

The crowd loved a surprise and they cheered in excitement as Tigris drove his chariot into the arena.

He was a large man of about forty-five and he looked dangerous. He wore silver armor and a silver tiger helmet with a face guard. The bright sun shone off his helmet as he rode around the arena with his arm held high. The crowd shouted and cheered even more loudly.

Tigris stopped his chariot, got down, and waited in the center of the arena. He was carrying a sword and a spear and he looked frightening.

When the crowd became quieter, Cassius started to speak again. "And from the great school of Aelius Proximo . . . Caesar is pleased to give you . . . the Spaniard, Maximus!"

There were more cheers and shouts from the crowd.

Maximus appeared from his gate. He was carrying only a short sword and a round silver shield. He had no armor or helmet.

Among the crowd that day were a group of people who did not usually go to watch gladiator games. They were soldiers from the Army of the North, with Valerius and Cicero at their center. They had come to see if it was true that their general was really still alive. When he got close enough for them to recognize him, they were very happy. They shouted to Maximus, but he could not hear their voices among so many others.

Commodus was also watching Maximus closely. "They love him like one of their own," he said to Lucilla.

"The crowd has its favorite for a time—then they find someone new. He'll be forgotten in a month," she replied.

"No," said Commodus, smiling. "Much sooner than that. It's been arranged."

Down on the arena sand, Maximus looked at Tigris. "Only one man with a sword and spear?" he thought. "Something's wrong. What don't I know?"

Maximus stopped a short distance from Tigris. They saluted each other, and then Tigris turned to the Emperor and raised his sword. "Before we die, we salute you," he said.

Maximus did not turn to the Emperor, or salute him. Instead, he bent down and picked up some sand, then let it run through his fingers.

Tigris pulled down the face guard on his helmet. Then he immediately attacked Maximus. Maximus struck back at him.

The two men were equal contestants—both strong and fast. Maximus was the younger man and he was very confident. He believed that he would not be killed that day.

As they fought, Maximus suddenly heard a strange noise. He could not understand where it was coming from. Then he felt the ground move.

Suddenly, a door opened in the sand behind him and an enormous tiger came out. It jumped at him. He felt the tiger's breath on his back as he moved quickly to one side, and he expected the animal to land on top of him. But when he looked, he saw that it was on the end of a long chain. This was held tightly by three men near the wall.

Tigris attacked again with great strength, forcing Maximus back toward the tiger. Maximus also attacked, and drove Tigris in a new direction. Then a second door opened in the sand, and another tiger jumped into the arena.

Maximus found a new position and continued to fight, as two more tigers suddenly appeared from the ground.

There were now four tigers, one in each corner of the battlefield. Maximus had five enemies to fight and he looked for a weak point.

Then it seemed that all four tigers were suddenly closer! Maximus realized what was happening. When Tigris was near a tiger, the men holding the chain pulled it in a little. When Maximus was near, they let the chain out further.

Finally, Maximus's strength and speed began to beat Tigris. He knocked Tigris back and they fell onto the sand together. Maximus quickly jumped to his feet and stood over him, his sword at his throat.

But then one of the teams of servants let go of the chain and a tiger ran at Maximus. He just had time to turn and push his sword upward into the tiger's shoulders. The animal fell on top of him and died. This gave Tigris enough time to get to his feet, pick up his sword, and prepare to attack again.

Maximus was under the heavy body of the dead tiger but he still had enough strength to throw his shield up at Tigris. It hit Tigris hard on the face guard of his helmet and bent it. It was impossible for him to see through it. Tigris was forced to drop his sword again so he could use both hands to try to pull the cover up.

Maximus was able to squeeze out from under the tiger and pick up Tigris's sword. The Frenchman was still blindly pulling at his helmet as Maximus knocked him to the ground.

Maximus stood over Tigris with his sword point at his throat. He looked to Commodus.

All eyes in the Colosseum turned to the Emperor.

Commodus was very angry but tried not to show it. He slowly stood and looked down at Maximus. He raised his arm and held out his hand—thumb down.

Maximus raised his sword to kill Tigris ... but suddenly threw it down on the sand, next to his head. "You fought with honor," he said.

The crowd was silent, then suddenly there was an enormous cheer. The shouts of "Maximus ... Maximus ..." grew louder and louder.

Commodus turned and disappeared from sight.

Senator Gracchus suddenly sat forward and started to take a real interest in the behavior of the crowd.

Maximus was almost at the gladiators' exit from the arena when a group of royal guards appeared in front of him. They stepped back as Commodus walked through them and toward the great fighter.

Maximus and Commodus stared at each other, just an arm's length away. The crowd was quiet now but they could not hear what was said.

"What am I going to do with you?" said Commodus.

Maximus did not reply.

"Once more I offer you my hand," Commodus said. He held out his arm, but Maximus did not move.

"Are we so different, you and I?" said Commodus. "You take life when you have to, just as I do."

"I have one more life to take," said Maximus. "Then it is finished."

"Then take it now," said Commodus.

Maximus knew he only had to take one step toward

Commodus and the guards would kill him. He turned his back on the Emperor and walked away.

The crowd went mad! They cheered Maximus, their hero. And then some started laughing at the Emperor and throwing bread at him.

Gracchus could not believe his eyes. Such insults to the Emperor usually resulted in death. But the people were not afraid now. All this, because of one brave man.

♦

Maximus and the gladiators were chained together again for the walk back to Proximo's school. There were guards walking with them, trying to keep back hundreds of people. They all wanted to get a close look at their hero.

Suddenly, Maximus heard a familiar voice and saw Cicero ahead in the crowd.

"Where are you camped?" he shouted to Cicero.

"A day's ride from Rome—at Ostia," replied Cicero. "We've been there all winter. The men are getting fat. They're bored."

"How soon could they be ready to fight?" asked Maximus.

"For you, sir? Tomorrow," Cicero said proudly.

The guards pushed Cicero back into the crowd. He ran ahead and came out in front of Maximus again, further along the street. This time he pushed a small package into Maximus's hand. The guards were close and Maximus knew he only had one chance.

"Cicero! Listen carefully!" he said. "You must contact Lucilla, the Emperor's sister. Tell her I will meet her politician."

There was no more time. Cicero disappeared into the crowd, and Maximus was forced to move on.

Later, alone in the prison at Proximo's school, Maximus took the little package out of his pocket and looked at it. Inside were the two wooden figures of his wife and son.

"Do they hear you?" a voice suddenly asked.

Maximus looked up into Juba's eyes.

"Your people," said Juba, "in the next world."

"Yes," said Maximus, looking down at the figures.

Juba thought about it. "What do you say to them?"

Maximus looked at his friend. "To my son, to keep his head up when he rides his horse," he said. "And to my wife ... that's private."

Juba smiled.

Chapter 10   Secrets and Lies

Commodus walked up and down in his room. He was a worried man. There was one other person with him: Senator Falco.

"An emperor cannot rule if he is not loved!" Commodus said to Falco. "And now they love Maximus because he let Tigris live. I can't kill him now or they will hate me. But I can't just let him continue like this—every day he adds another insult. It's like a bad dream."

"Every day his power is greater," said Falco. "And the people are getting braver. The Senate sees it, too. This is not something that will go away in a few days or weeks. Rome is beginning to move against you. He must die."

"Then they will love him even more!" shouted Commodus. He began walking again and soon he was calmer. "When I went to the Senate today," he said, "I purposely told them about selling the wheat to pay for the games. And what happened?"

"Nothing," said Falco.

"Exactly! Nothing!" said Commodus. "Even Gracchus was as silent as a mouse. Why?" He stopped and looked out his window over Rome.

"We must be quiet and patient, Caesar. We must let the enemy come to us," said Falco.

Commodus began to relax a little. "Have every senator followed," he ordered. "I want daily reports."

◆

It was easy to find Lucilla, but much harder to speak to her. For two days Cicero stayed in the streets around the palace. Finally, he was lucky. Lucilla's carriage came toward him, surrounded by royal guards. There were two other men following her carriage— but they were not in uniform. One, a small man, was blind in one eye. He was one of Falco's secret police. He had been very good at watching senators, but now he had been given a different job. He was watching Lucilla.

As the carriage passed, Cicero called out, "My lady! I served your father at Vindobona!" Lucilla heard but did not pay him much attention. The guards pushed him away, and he ran around to the other side of the carriage. "And I served General Maximus!" he said, when he got close enough.

Lucilla called for her carriage to stop. She asked her servant for a coin and held it out to Cicero. "And I serve him still," he said, as he came closer to take it.

Lucilla understood at once that he was a messenger. She told her guards to step back. "This is for your loyalty, soldier," she said.

Cicero took the coin and kissed her hand. He whispered, "A message from the General. He'll meet your politician."

It was enough. Cicero stepped back into the crowd, and Lucilla's carriage moved on.

◆

Proximo's school was dark and quiet. The men were all asleep, except one. Proximo went quietly to wake Maximus and then took him to his own rooms.

Lucilla and Gracchus were there, waiting for Maximus.

Proximo turned and left immediately. Lucilla introduced Gracchus to Maximus.

"The Senate is with you?" asked Maximus.

"The Senate? Yes, I can speak for them," Gracchus replied.

"Can you buy my freedom and get me out of Rome?" asked Maximus, wasting no time.

"Why would I do that?"

"Get me out of the city. Have fresh horses ready to take me to Ostia. My army is camped there. By the second night, I'll be back with 5,000 men," said Maximus.

"But there are new commanders," said Lucilla. "Loyal to Commodus."

"Let my men see me alive. They are still loyal to *me*."

"This is crazy," said Gracchus. "No Roman army has entered the city in 100 years. This may be no better than the rule of Commodus. And what next? After the battle to take control of Rome you'll take your men and just . . . leave?"

"I will leave," said Maximus. "The soldiers will stay to protect you, under the command of the Senate."

"When all of Rome is yours, you'll just give it back to the people?" asked Gracchus. "Tell me why."

"Because that was the last wish of a dying man," said Maximus, quietly. "I will kill Commodus and leave Rome to you."

There was silence, then Gracchus spoke again. "Marcus Aurelius trusted you, his daughter trusts you. So I will trust you, too. Give me two days." He held out his hand to Maximus. "And stay alive."

◆

In his beautiful house Senator Gracchus listened to the cheers coming from the Colosseum. His servant helped him pack a large amount of money into a bag.

"Wait outside the Colosseum. He'll come to you," he told the man.

Gracchus's servant left the house and walked toward the Colosseum. All the way he was followed by one of Falco's secret police.

Proximo sat in a café and waited. He seemed to be watching the crowd passing, but really he was looking for Gracchus's servant. He knew immediately when he saw him, but just continued drinking his wine. He looked up and down the street.

Suddenly, he saw a man standing by a door and he did not like the look of him. It was Falco's one-eyed secret policeman.

Gracchus's servant stood patiently for a long time with his bag of money, but no one came to him. In the café Proximo's table was now empty. He knew when to disappear.

♦

Maximus was brought to Proximo's room by two guards just after sunset. He was impatient, ready to start. Proximo looked at Maximus and shook his head. "I tried," he said. "It won't work. The Emperor knows too much. And this has become too dangerous for me."

"Let me go," said Maximus, "and you'll be paid when I return. I promise you."

"And what will happen if you don't return?" asked Proximo.

"Trust me—I will kill Commodus," said Maximus.

Proximo looked hard at Maximus, studying him.

"I know I can trust you, General," he said. "I know you would die for honor, or for Rome, or the memory of your family. I, on the other hand, am just an entertainer." He called for his guards. "Take him away."

Maximus looked straight into Proximo's eyes. "He killed the man who freed you," he said.

After Maximus had gone, Proximo picked up the wooden

sword that Marcus Aurelius had given him, the sign of his freedom. And he thought for a long time.

◆

Falco's spies were good at their job. They had followed Gracchus and the other senators, then Lucilla, and now Proximo. Lucilla knew their lives were in great danger and she tried to keep her brother calm.

Maximus also knew it. Commodus would come for him soon, he was certain. In the dark of night in his prison room, he suddenly heard footsteps coming toward him.

It was Proximo. He woke Juba and threw him out. Then he turned to Maximus. "Congratulations, General," he said. "You have very good friends." He stepped back and Lucilla came into the room. Proximo left them together.

"My brother plans to put Gracchus in prison," she said. "We can't wait any longer. You must leave tonight. Proximo will come for you at midnight and take you to a gate. Cicero will be there with horses."

"You've done all this? You're very brave, Lucilla."

"I am tired of being brave," she said. "My brother hates everyone—and you most of all."

"Because your father chose me."

"No," she said. "Because my father loved you ... and I loved you."

Maximus took her hands in his.

"I've felt alone all my life—except with you," she said.

She turned to go, but Maximus held her and they kissed. It was their first kiss for many years, and, for a short time, they rested in each other's arms.

They separated, with one last look, and Lucilla went quickly back into the dark night.

◆

Back in the palace, Lucilla hurried to her son's bedroom. She looked around and called to the servant. "Where is Lucius?"

"He's with the Emperor, my lady," she replied

Lucilla rushed down the palace halls, looking in all the rooms she passed. Finally, in great fear, she opened her brother's door.

Commodus and Lucius were sitting together, looking at some papers. "Sister, come and join us," said Commodus, smiling. A frightening smile. "I've been reading to dear Lucius about the great Julius Caesar." He took Lucius on his knee. "And tomorrow, if you're very good, I'll tell you the story of the Emperor Claudius," he said. Commodus looked right into Lucilla's eyes. "He trusted the people closest to him, but they didn't deserve his trust."

Lucilla felt faint. She sat down opposite them.

"The Emperor knew they had been very busy, planning against him," Commodus went on, watching his sister's terror all the time. "And one night he sat down with one of them and said to her, 'Tell me what you have planned, or I shall kill the person you love the most. You will see me wash in their blood.'"

Lucilla kept her eyes on her son, and a tear ran down her face.

"And the Emperor's heart was broken because she had wounded him more than anyone else could. And what do you think happened next, Lucius?"

"I don't know, Uncle," said Lucius, nervously.

"She told him everything," Commodus said.

Chapter 11   Broken Plans

The sound of marching feet broke the silence of night in the area around the Colosseum.

In his room Proximo was packing his bags, planning to leave Rome fast. He heard the marching feet coming toward the school and he knew then how he was going to die. He picked up his bunch of keys and hurried across to the prison rooms. He was almost there when the royal guards arrived and stopped in front of his gates.

"Open up in the name of the Emperor!" the captain called out loudly. For a few seconds Proximo paused, without turning to look at them. Then he continued toward the prisons.

Maximus had also heard the marching feet and knew their meaning exactly. He watched as Proximo appeared through the prison entrance, keys in hand.

"Everything is ready," said Proximo. He handed the keys to Maximus. "It seems you've won your freedom."

"Proximo," said Maximus, as he took the keys, "are you in danger of becoming a good man?"

Proximo walked back to his rooms. The guards could see him through the gates, but he did not look across at them once.

"The Emperor commands you to open these gates, Proximo!" shouted the captain. "Do you want to die, old man? Tonight all enemies of the Emperor must die!" Proximo walked on, and up the stairs to his room. "Break the locks!" shouted the captain.

◆

Maximus quickly unlocked his door. Then he and Juba let Haken and the others out.

The sound of metal hitting metal came from the gates. Maximus knew he had to go, now. He handed the bunch of keys to Juba.

Juba took them, understanding. "Go!" he said.

The gates to Proximo's school flew open and the guards rushed in. Maximus ran for the back entrance. Juba, Haken, and the other gladiators threw themselves between the guards and Maximus and slowed them down enough for him to get away. By the back entrance Maximus found his army sword and armor waiting for him.

In the fighting, Juba was knocked to the ground and left for dead. Haken was first wounded by a Roman sword and then shot through the chest with four arrows. His enormous body fell, dead, at the bottom of the stairs.

The guards climbed over Haken's body and raced up to Proximo's room. When they broke through the door, they found him at his desk with his back to them. In his hand was the wooden sword Marcus Aurelius had given him with his freedom. He did not turn to see death coming. The end came quickly, with three deep wounds to his neck and back. He died with the wooden sword hanging at his side, held tightly in his hand.

♦

Maximus came out of the back entrance to the school and waited quietly in the shadows. Suddenly, he heard a horse move. He looked toward the sound and moved out into the street. There were two horses waiting, one with a rider. As he got closer, he could see that it was Cicero.

But something felt wrong. Maximus hid behind some rocks and whispered Cicero's name.

Cicero turned. "Maximus!" he shouted. "No!"

As he shouted, his horse suddenly ran and Cicero was pulled from it by a rope around his neck. He was left hanging from the tree above.

Maximus rushed forward and caught him by the legs. At the same time six arrows flew into Cicero's chest, killing him immediately.

Maximus had his sword ready. But there were too many guards and he had no chance.

A voice called out, "Take him alive!" and the guards quickly caught him, making him a prisoner again.

♦

At sunrise, even before their servants were awake, Senator Gaius and his wife were murdered in their bed by royal guards. Seven other senators were killed the same morning, also many private citizens. All these people had upset Commodus in some way. His secret police had done a good job.

Senator Gracchus was not killed, but the guards took him away from his home and threw him into prison.

In his room at the palace Falco came to tell Commodus the news. Commodus was pleased that so many of his enemies were finished. After Falco had gone, he spoke to Lucilla.

"Lucius will stay with me now," he said, walking across the room toward her. "And if his mother even looks at me in a way that upsets me, he will die. If she decides to take her own life, he will die." He smiled and touched her hair. "Kiss me, sister," he said.

◆

It was hot and dusty in the Colosseum. Hundreds of servants at the top of the arena were throwing red flowers down onto the sand. Fifty-five thousand Romans were waiting. They had been told to expect something special.

Maximus was also waiting. He knew there was only death ahead of him. But he still hoped for a soldier's death, and he kept his back straight and his head up. On his way to the arena he passed a prison room where Juba and Proximo's other gladiators were. When he saw Maximus, Juba stood in a silent salute to a brave man and a friend.

Under the floor of the Colosseum arena was a large elevator, operated by servants with ropes. It was the way the tigers had entered the arena when Maximus fought Tigris.

Maximus was led there now by Quintus and the royal guards. They fastened his chains to the elevator and Quintus himself checked them. As he bent to do this he whispered softly, "I'm a soldier. I obey."

Someone was walking toward them. Quintus stood up again and moved back. Emperor Commodus suddenly appeared with a group of servants carrying armor. The Emperor himself was wearing his own gold armor. He wore this armor when he wanted to feel like a god.

Commodus and six of his guards joined Maximus on the elevator. Maximus expected to die immediately, but Commodus smiled at him.

"Listen to the crowd," he said. "They are calling for you. The general who became a slave. The slave who became a gladiator. The gladiator who insulted an emperor." He called his servants forward with the armor. "It's a good story," he said. "And now the people want to know how the story ends. Only a great death will be good enough," Commodus continued. "And what could be better than to fight the Emperor himself in the greatest arena?"

Maximus did not believe him. "You will fight me?"

"Why not?" Commodus said. "Do you think I'm afraid?"

The servants began to fix armor to Maximus's body, first his arms, legs, and shoulders. They left the body armor until last.

"I think you've been afraid all your life," Maximus answered. He knew Commodus would never have a fair fight with him. What would he do to make sure he won?

"Unlike Maximus the Brave, who knows no fear?" said Commodus.

"I've been afraid. But you took away from me everything I loved. Since then, you're right, I have not known fear," said Maximus.

"There is one thing left—you still have your life to lose," said Commodus.

"I once knew a man who said, 'Death smiles at us all. A man can only smile back,'" said Maximus.

"I wonder," said Commodus, "did your friend smile at his own death?"

"You must know," Maximus replied. "He was your father."

Commodus was silent, and they stared at each other.

"You loved my father, I know," Commodus said. "But I did, too. That makes us brothers, doesn't it?" He reached out his arms to Maximus and put them around him.

Maximus suddenly let out a cry of pain. The Emperor had a small, sharp knife in his hand. He had wounded Maximus in the side, cutting him deeply.

"Smile for me now, brother," Commodus said, as he pulled the knife out. Quintus stared, shocked. "Now put on his body armor. Hide the wound," Commodus said to his servants.

◆

All eyes in the Colosseum watched the center of the arena as the elevator came up. Commodus stepped off and onto the sand. It was covered with red flowers.

Commodus took his sword from Quintus and turned slowly to all sides of the arena. Maximus stood straight, but he was in great pain. He looked up to the royal seats and saw Lucilla there with Lucius and Senator Gracchus. They were surrounded by guards.

Commodus raised his sword high and the sun shone off it.

Maximus slowly bent down and picked up some sand from the arena. Quintus threw Maximus's sword down on the ground near his feet. Maximus picked it up, slowly, and stood facing the Emperor. And the fight began.

Commodus rushed at Maximus and knocked him to the ground. Maximus got to his feet with difficulty. The arena seemed to be turning around. The sun danced off the Emperor's armor and blinded him. He heard the noise of the crowd—now it seemed to be far away, now close.

Standing behind the entrance, Juba saw a thin line of blood running out from under Maximus's armor.

Lucilla watched him in fear. He seemed to be looking straight at her. Could he see her? She held out her hand and called his name.

Commodus struck him again. Then he raised his arms to the crowd. One or two people shouted, "Commodus!" The crowd loved a winner.

Maximus almost fell again. The sun was bright, very bright. And then suddenly, beyond all this, he saw the sun shining on a pink wall ... He saw a gate in the wall ... and a field of apple trees beyond it ...

He pushed himself forward and, as he did so, he struck Commodus. The crowd cheered.

Commodus came forward again and knocked Maximus back to the ground. The crowd were silent. Only the sound of the two men could be heard.

Maximus saw something else now ... A woman stood in the doorway of a pink stone house ... There was a field of wheat behind the house ...

Commodus stood over Maximus with his sword ready for the kill.

"Maximus!" One person in the crowd called out in the silence.

Commodus looked around, angrily. The crowd repeated the cry. "Maximus!" Commodus turned back and brought his sword down.

But the sound of the crowd had brought Maximus back to the arena and given him new strength. He pushed his sword up and knocked Commodus's sword away. Suddenly he got to his feet and attacked the Emperor, forcing him back. The crowd cheered loudly.

Then Maximus saw an opportunity and pushed his sword forward. It caught Commodus under his arm and he dropped his sword.

Commodus called to Quintus. "Give me your sword!"

But Quintus just stared through him.

Commodus turned to the guards. "A sword! Give me a sword!"

Some started to come forward, but Quintus stopped them. "Put your swords away!" he ordered.

Commodus looked around, suddenly frightened. He saw the great crowd and heard the name of his enemy on all sides.

"Maximus! Maximus! Maximus!" they shouted. Senators joined in the cry. Juba and the gladiators shouted the name, too.

Lucilla stood in silence, her hand to her mouth.

But Maximus was dying. He could not stand. He dropped his own sword. He seemed to be reaching out toward something . . . a pink stone wall with a gate . . . a wheat field . . . the sound of a child's laugh . . .

Commodus saw Maximus fall to his knees and he stood over him. He took the small knife in his hand again and lifted it, ready to strike Maximus one last time.

Maximus saw the knife coming toward him. He held Commodus's arm and pulled him onto the ground. Suddenly finding power from somewhere, Maximus turned the knife around and pushed it deep into Commodus's neck.

There was a look of surprise on the Emperor's face, then he took one last breath and died.

Maximus slowly stood, took one step forward, and reached out a hand. Quintus went to him. "Maximus . . ."

"Quintus, free my men," said Maximus.

The crowd was completely quiet.

Maximus saw his own hand on the gate, pushing it open . . . Walking away from him was a woman, and a child running . . . They looked back and smiled at him . . .

Maximus fell to the sand.

Out of the silence, Lucilla crossed the arena to the place where he lay. She took him in her arms. She could see that she could not save him, but she wanted him to hear her before the end.

"Maximus," Lucilla said softly.

Maximus's dying eyes opened again. "Lucius is safe?" he asked.

"Yes."

"Our sons live."

Lucilla smiled. "Our sons live. And they are proud." She kissed him, crying, and whispered, "Go to them. You're home."

Maximus walked through the wheat field … The beautiful woman stopped and turned. She called to the boy. He stopped running and looked back. The boy then started running back along the road, toward the man in the wheat field, toward his father, who was coming home at last.

Maximus died in Lucilla's arms, as she placed him gently on the sand. When she stood up, the whole arena was watching her. She turned and spoke to the senators. "Rome is free again," she said.

Lucilla stood over Maximus's body as Gracchus and the senators came down onto the sand.

"He was a soldier of Rome," Lucilla said. "Honor him."

Quintus's voice rang out, "Free the prisoners!"

A hand turned a key, and Juba led the last of Proximo's gladiators into the silent arena.

Gracchus stood by the body. "Who will help me carry this man?"

A few voices broke the silence, calling Maximus's name. Then many more voices joined in. The sound grew and filled the arena.

The gladiators picked Maximus up on their shoulders. Silent and proud, following Gracchus and the other senators in a slow march, they carried him out of the arena.

Lucilla stood for a long time, watching them go, while her mad brother lay dead on the bloody sand behind her.

Chapter 12 Home, At Last

The games had ended.

The Colosseum was empty and silent as Juba walked across the sand. Juba, now dressed in his African clothes, was a free man again. And soon he was going home.

He still heard one voice in the arena, though. He heard Maximus, the great fighter, asking about his home in Africa and talking to him about his own home in Spain.

Juba moved to the center of the arena and found the exact place he was looking for: a small area of blood on the sand. He dropped to his knees and made a little hole in the ground. He took something from his pocket—the small wooden figures of Maximus's wife and son.

He carefully put them in the hole and covered them with the earth that carried their loved one's blood. Now it would be easier for them to find each other in the next world.

"Now we are free," he said loudly, looking around at the empty, silent arena. "This place will become dust, but I will not forget you."

He stood above the place where Maximus had died. "I will see you again," he said to his friend. He smiled the wide smile that he had smiled for Maximus in life and would soon smile for his own wife and daughters. "But not yet."

He walked slowly out of the arena, looking back just once at the place, as the wind blew red flowers across the killing ground.

ACTIVITIES

Chapters 1–3

Before you read

1 Find the word *empire* in your dictionary. Was your country once part of the Roman Empire? Was it part of another great empire? Did it have a different name then?

2 Check the meaning of these words in your dictionary. They are all used in this story. Then answer the questions.

armor   arrow   emperor   general   gladiator   republic   slave
senate   shield   sword

a Which four words are for people?
b Which two things can you use to kill someone?
c Which two things would protect you in a fight?
d Which two words tell you about the government of a country?

3 Now check the meanings of these words. Choose the best words to complete the sentences below.

battle   carriage   cheer   glory   honor   raise   salute   swing
train   trap   wheat   wound

a Many soldiers were killed in the . . . . . and many more were . . . . . .
b The winners . . . . . their arms, and the crowd . . . . . .
c When a soldier passes an officer, he must . . . . . him.
d We drove in our . . . . . past fields of . . . . . .
e There were enemy soldiers all around me—I was . . . . . .
f He's new here, so they will . . . . . him to do the job.
g "Don't . . . . . that ladder around! You'll break a window."
h "We . . . . . all those soldiers who died for the . . . . . of Rome!"

After you read

4 Answer these questions:
a Why does Commodus think his father is really sick?
b What does Maximus do to show that he is ready for battle?
c Why do you think the Roman army wins the battle?
d How does Commodus feel about Maximus?
e What does Marcus want Maximus to become and why?

5 Are these sentences true or false? Correct the false ones.

 a Quintus is woken in the middle of the night by Maximus.

 b Maximus realizes that Marcus has been killed by Commodus.

 c Quintus believes that the Emperor died of natural causes.

 d Cornelius takes Maximus down into the trees to kill him.

 e Maximus is wounded with a cut to his neck.

Chapters 4–6

Before you read

6 Discuss these questions.

 a Where do you think Maximus will go? Why?

 b Do you think Quintus will try to help him? Why (not)?

7 Check the meanings of these words in your dictionary.

arena   cage   chain   spear   tiger

Which is:

 a something that is sharp, pointed and could kill a man?

 b something that you use to stop an animal running away?

 c a prison for an animal?

 d a wild animal?

 e a place where sports and games are held?

After you read

8 Who says these things? Who to? What are they talking about?

 a "They're more expensive than we are."

 b "Some are good for fighting, some for dying. You need both."

 c "Tomorrow you can scream in seven languages."

 d "You go out into the arena as slaves. You come back—if you come back—as gladiators."

9 Explain:

 a Senator Gracchus's opinion of Commodus.

 b how Commodus first gets the idea for the gladiator games.

 c why Commodus thinks the games are a good idea.

10 Who are these people? What do you know about them?

 a He is a large man with big, blue eyes, white hair, and a white beard.

b He is small, and looks quite ordinary, but he only has one eye.

c He is a tall, thin man with long hair.

Chapters 7–9

Before you read

11 Who do you think the spy is selling his information to? What do you think will happen to him?

12 Check the meanings of these words in your dictionary.

chariot   helmet

    a Add one of the words to each of these groups:

       sword/shield/armor/ . . . . .

       horse/wheels/driver/ . . . . .

    b Now write a sentence containing both words.

After you read

13 Answer these questions.

    a Why does Proximo tell Maximus, "Remember, you're an entertainer!"?

    b Why is Maximus suddenly interested in Proximo's advice?

    c Why is Proximo unhappy about his gladiators acting the Battle of Carthage?

14 Work with another student. After Lucius meets "the Spaniard," he tells his mother about it. Act out the conversation.

15 Where do these people meet? Why?

    a Lucilla and Gaius (chapter 7)

    b Commodus and Maximus (chapter 8)

    c Maximus and Lucilla (chapter 8)

    d Maximus and Cicero (chapter 9)

Chapters 10–12

Before you read

16 Discuss how the story will end for:

    a Maximus   **b** Commodus   **c** Lucilla   **d** Rome

After you read

17 Answer these questions.

   a What does Commodus tell Falco that he must do to get more
      information?

   b Why doesn't Proximo meet Gracchus's servant?

   c Why does Commodus tell Lucius the story of Emperor
      Claudius?

18 Put these events in the right order. The royal guards are outside
   Proximo's school.

   a The guards rush in through the gates.

   b Haken is killed.

   c The captain shouts, "Break the locks!"

   d Proximo is killed.

   e Maximus hears the guards coming to the school.

   f Maximus gives the keys to Juba.

   g The guards run up to Proximo's room.

   h Proximo gives the keys to Maximus.

19 Discuss how you felt at the end of the story. Was it the right
   ending? Why (not)?

Writing

20 Imagine you are Lucilla. After the last fight in the Colosseum you
   must explain to Lucius why both men died. Write your conversation
   with Lucius.

21 It is the day after the death of Maximus. Write a report for Rome's
   English-language newspaper about his death. Tell your readers
   what happened in the Colosseum.

22 It is the day after the spy has heard the senators talking in the café.
   Now he must give the information to Senator Falco. Write his report.

23 What does Maximus mean when he asks Proximo, "Are you in
   danger of becoming a good man?"? What do we know about
   Proximo? What is your opinion of him?

24 It is a year after the end of the story. What do you think has
   happened in that time? How has life changed for Lucilla, Gracchus,

and Quintus? Are the people of Rome happier or are they unhappy with the republic?

25 Did you enjoy the book? Write a short report for someone who has not read it. If you have also seen the movie, compare this to the book. Why do you think the movie was so popular?

Answers for the Activities in this book are published in our free resource packs for teachers, the Penguin Readers Factsheets, or available on a separate sheet. Please write to your local Pearson Education office or to: Marketing Department, Penguin Longman Publishing, 5 Bentinck Street, London W1M 5RN.